THE MAGICAL FLUTIST

Exercises for
Tone and Technique

About the Author

Katri Rehnström (b. Seinäjoki, Finland, 1979) is a Finnish musician and flute teacher. She has completed bachelor's degrees in Classical Piano Pedagogy, Classical Flute Pedagogy and Pop & Jazz Flute Pedagogy. Katri has been teaching the flute and improvisation at music schools in Finland, for example, teaching improvisation to classical flute teachers. Recently she has been working as a freelance flutist in Finland and as a writer of music education material. She has published two improvisation books entitled *Improkatin ABC* (2023) and *Sävel on vapaa!* (2013) with Annika Gummerus-Putkinen. Katri hopes *The Magical Flutist* will be an inspiring daily practice book for flutists and flute teachers around the world.

THE MAGICAL FLUTIST

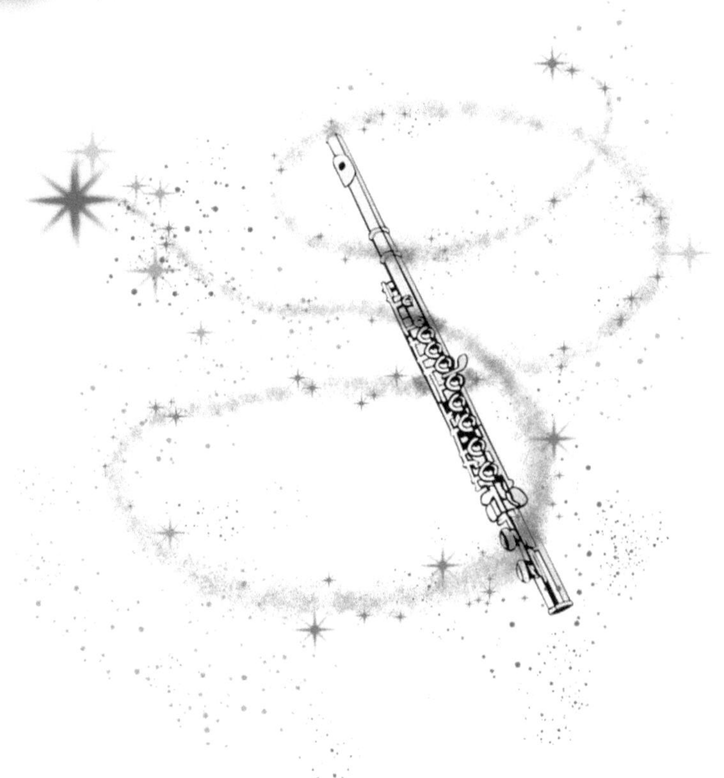

Exercises for Tone and Technique

Katri Rehnström

Notation Editing: Seppo Rehnström
Cover and Layout Design: Seppo Rehnström
Illustrations: Katri and Seppo Rehnström

English Translation: Wilja Rosenberg (pp. 8-64) and Heini Ernamo (pp. 65-107)
English Proofreading: Sarka Hantula

Original Title: *Huiluvelhon käsikirja - Kootut harjoitukset*
Originally published in Helsinki, Finland, in 2021 by the author
Finnish Proofreading: Raija Järventausta
Publisher: BoD · Books on Demand, Mannerheimintie 12 B, 00100 Helsinki,
bod@bod.fi
Print: Libri Plureos GmbH, Friedensallee 273, 22763 Hamburg, Germany
ISBN: 978-952-80-7127-3

Acknowledgements

I would like to thank the Finnish Cultural Foundation, Arts Promotion Center
Finland and the Seinäjoki Town Council Cultural Services for the financial
support of this work. I am also grateful to Rainer Risberg,
James Robert Hopkins, Raija and Lasse Järventausta, Silja Järventausta, Hanna
Järventausta, Marja-Leena Rosenberg as well as my colleagues and friends for
their advice, comments, ideas and inspiration.

Katri Rehnström

Contents:

Preface

The *Magical Flutist — Exercises for Tone and Technique* was inspired by the tuition of the Finnish flute pedagogue Rainer Risberg. This book brings the exercises and instructions as close to practice as possible. *The Magical Flutist* includes detailed instructions, various exercises, and useful images for improving your tone and technique. The exercises have been organized thematically, so that you can build your practice sessions by picking and choosing exercises from different chapters to suit your needs.

For clarity purposes, the exercises have not been written in all keys. It is recommendable to transpose them into different keys, including the relative minor keys. Learners can transpose the exercises by ear or write them on the blank staff at the end of the book. Approximate tempo markings can be adjusted to the learner's skill level to ease or increase the challenge. *The Magical Flutist — Exercises for Tone and Technique* can be used as teaching material in flute lessons. It is also well suited for an intermediate level self-study.

The idea of this book was born while I was studying towards my bachelor's degree in Classical Flute Pedagogy at the Lahti University of Applied Sciences, Finland, from 2012 to 2016. Because of the closing of the Music and Drama Department and the approaching retirement of Rainer Risberg, I wanted to preserve the exact spirit and approach to flute playing I had enjoyed so much in Rainer Risberg's lessons. The book was also strongly inspired by my own musical path. As I began playing the flute as a secondary instrument in my twenties, I was looking for an intermediate level flute school that would give me a proper introduction to the world of flute playing and help me to practice independently. This book draws on the insights of the wonderful flute pedagogue Rainer Risberg and my own research and discoveries. The legacy of the flute wizard lives on, reminding us that playing the flute is... easy!

Kuortane, Finland, May 2024
Katri Rehnström

Flute Tree

Embouchure
Breathing
Tonguing
Posture
Articulation
Finger Gymnastics
Registers
Vibrato
Flexibility
Nuances
Tone Color
Intonation

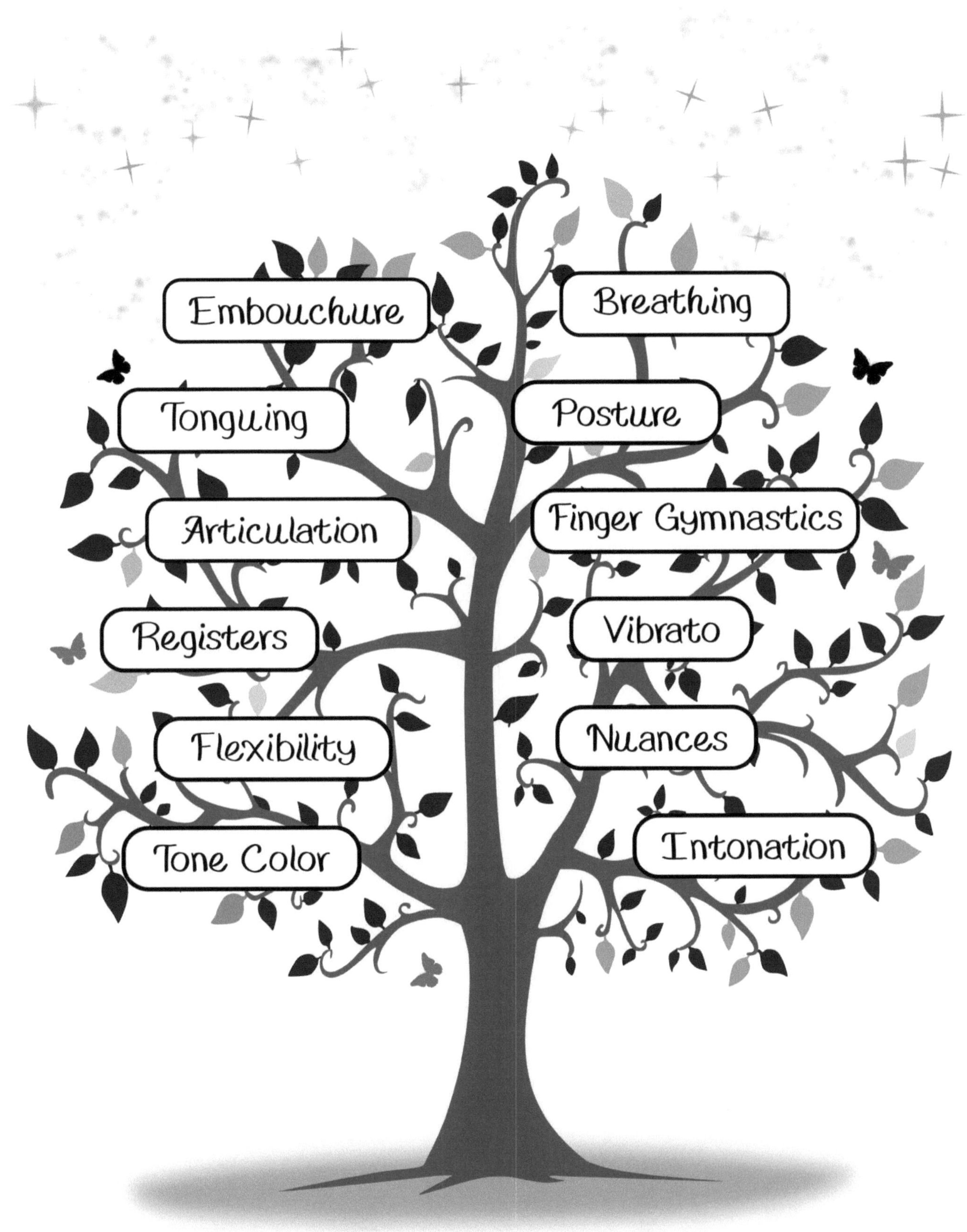

Practice Journal

Date ________________

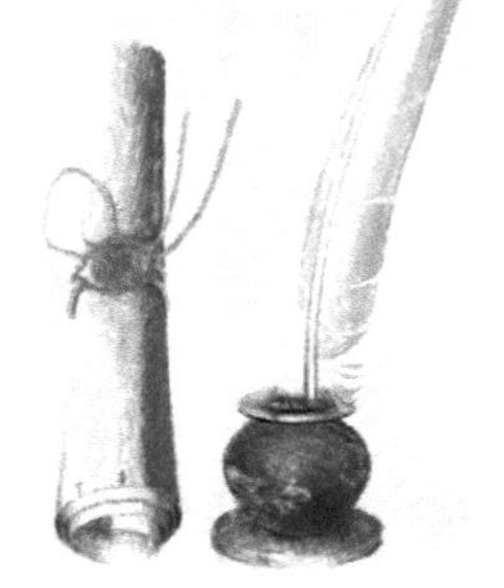

Tone and
Technique ____

Etudes ____

Repertoire ____

Body Care ____

Note to Self ____

1

Embouchure

Useful Images

You can observe your own embouchure and the alignment of the head joint in relation to the lips with the help of a mirror. While blowing, don't let the lips spread into a smile or tuck over the teeth. Imagine that there is a small air bubble behind the lips as if you were saying 'pew' but leave out the /j/ sound after the /p/. See how the upper lip forms a tiny beak.

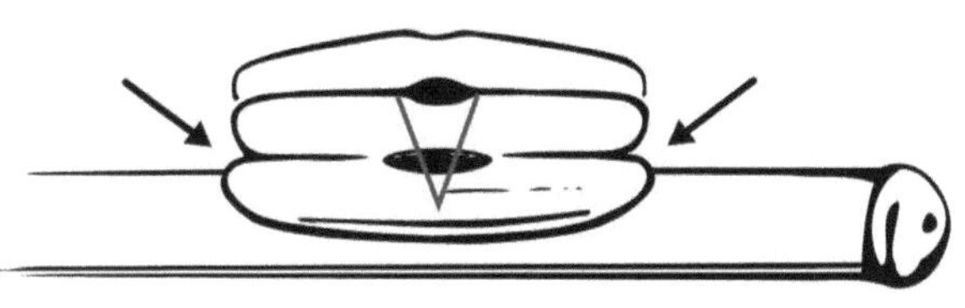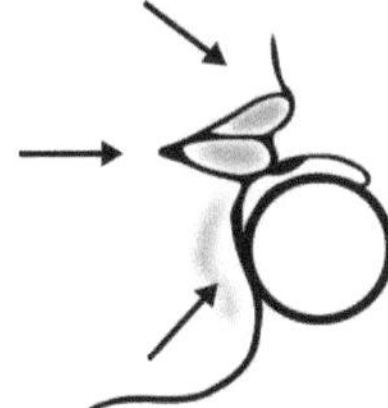

- ♦ Think of smiling without smiling.
- ♦ Control the lip aperture: don't let it get too wide and flat.
- ♦ Experiment with different imaginary lip apertures.

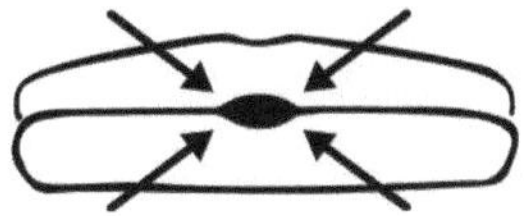

The ü position

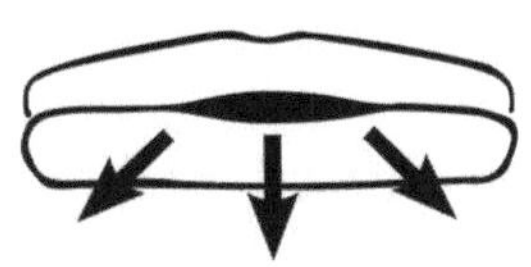

Avoid

While playing, the lip aperture and the air column tend to widen. You can narrow the lip aperture by contracting and puckering the corners of the mouth slightly. In other words, we don't make the aperture smaller by stretching the corners of the mouth towards the ears, as we do when smiling.

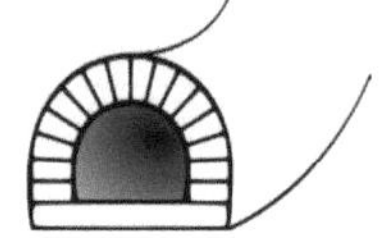

The upper and lower lip support each other in the direction of the airstream, similarly to a drainpipe directing water.

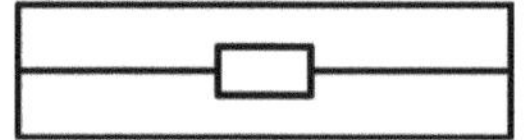

A mental image of the lip aperture having a clear shape and distinct edges.

A mental image of a zipper helps us to seal the edges of the lip aperture.

Test it

♦ Move the lip aperture one millimeter to the left and then to the right from what you are accustomed to.
♦ Seal one corner of the mouth and open the other simultaneously.
♦ Gently puff out one cheek, then the other.
♦ Stretch the lower lip by about a millimeter to the left / to the right.
♦ Move the flute a millimeter to the left then to the right.

(Herbert Lindholm: *Flautissimo, Pedagoginen Huilukansio* 1985.)

When aligning the head joint and the body, it's important to ensure a good position for the hands and wrists. The keys should face the ceiling (or even slightly outwards). If the keys of the flute turn inwards, the angle of the right-hand wrist will cause tension and strain. Then again, if the keys of the flute turn too far outwards, the left wrist will get strained.

Exercises

Lips Follow the Flute - An Exercise with the Flute

With the help of this exercise, you can find the optimal position for the lips, the perfect angle of the airstream and a focused sound while staying relaxed.

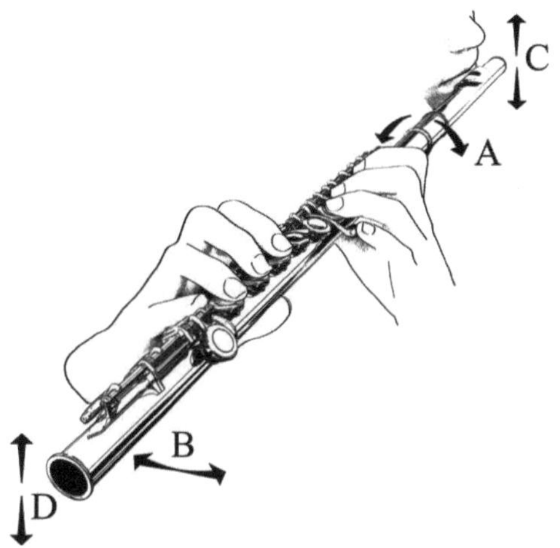

A) Turn the flute outwards and inwards alternately.
B) Gently push the tail of the flute forward with your right hand. Follow the flute with your lips.
C) Lift and lower the chin.
D) Lift and lower the tail of the flute.

Light Workout

a) Imagine you scoop something up with the lower lip, so that the lower lip scoops up and swipes over the upper lip.
b) Turn the corners of the mouth down and pout, as if you were displeased.
c) Move the upper lip up and down like a rabbit.

Stick Relaxation

Hang matchsticks, drinking straws or something similar from the corners of your mouth. Use minimal traction to hold the sticks or straws in place. Try to play something simple on the flute, for example, part of a scale, with a grip that is as relaxed as possible. Also try to move the sticks closer to each other, to the place where your canine teeth are. If the embouchure starts to tire while playing a piece, recall the relaxed feeling of this exercise!

Stirring Stick

Place a stirring stick lightly between the lips and let the embouchure form around it. Remove the stick and blow a long 'pew' without the /j/ sound. The stick helps you to pucker the lips slightly. You can also make use of a drinking straw. Breathe calmly and blow a long and even airstream through the straw.

Zooming with Tape

Place pieces of adhesive tape on top of the edges of the flute embouchure hole. The tapes narrow the hole of the lip plate by a few millimeters on both sides. Try to play part of a scale in the middle register. If the lip aperture is too big while playing, try zooming with the help of "imaginary tapes". Clean the lip plate gently after removing the tapes.

Check

♦ Check your facial expressions in a mirror while playing and not playing. Do you see any unnecessary wrinkles while you play?

2

Tone Exercises

Basics

A beautiful sound is

The first exercises are played mostly without the tongue, so that the air flows freely and swiftly. In order to acquire deep sound, imagine the lowest possible starting point for the blow, in the pelvis, in the thighs and even in the ground below your feet.

Check in the mirror that the shoulders remain relaxed and down during inhalation. Imagine that the head and neck are like a big, booming bell: the wider the space, the bigger the sound. Imagine that the chin is hollow and the root of the tongue rests on the base of the mouth.

Relaxed Warm-up

Beautifully Booming, Hauntingly Hollow

- Imagine there is a big cave at the pit of your stomach. Fill the cave with your inhalation.
- When you breathe in, relax the chin and the abdomen.
- Imagine the air flowing in through an opening in the lower back.
- Get the air moving and feel the airstream during inhalation and exhalation.

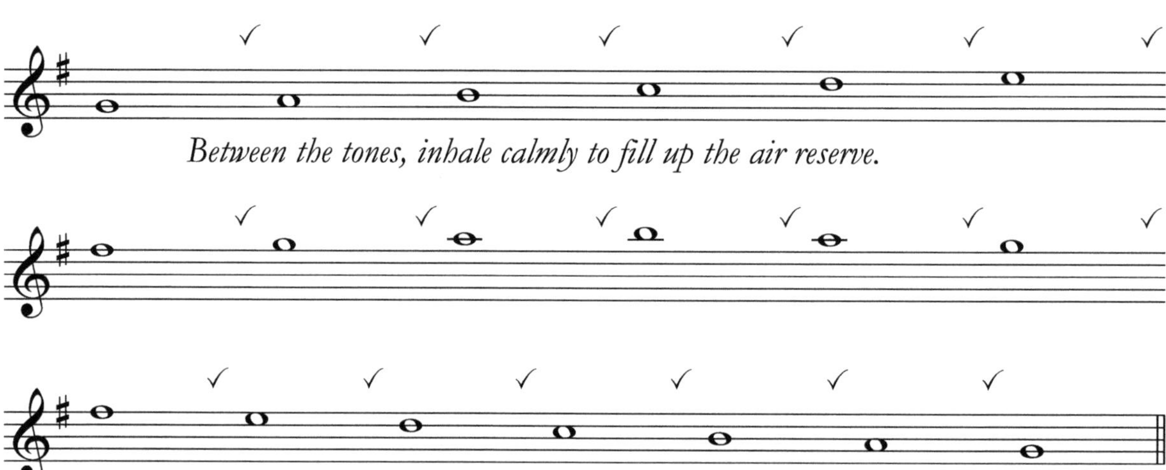

Between the tones, inhale calmly to fill up the air reserve.

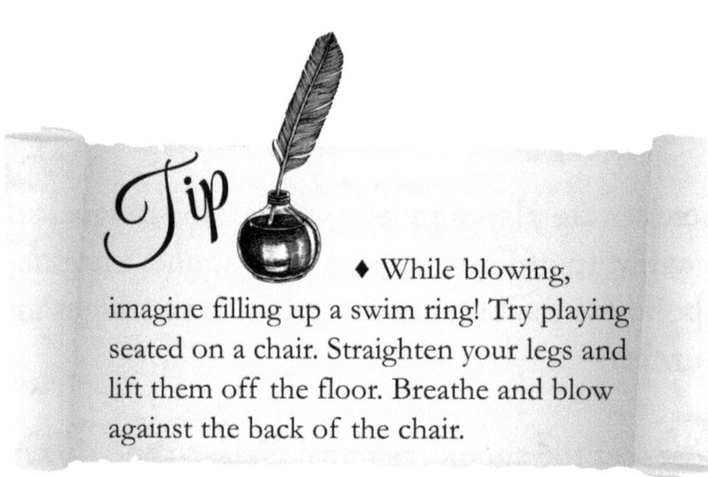

Preparing the Sound in Slow Motion

- ♦ Starting with natural deep breathing →
  relaxing the abs and the jaw
- ♦ A delicate preparation of the embouchure and the lip aperture
- ♦ Blowing a focused and steady airstream
- ♦ A clear onset and an effortless sound

Useful Symbols:

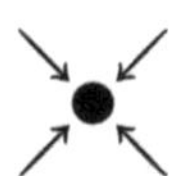
The corners of the mouth are brought forward. This helps you to transition to higher registers.

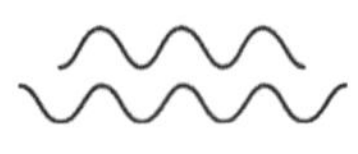
Do the duck face. Lips protrude and the inner parts of the lips are brought against each other.

Add real emotion and passion into your playing!

The Three Cornerstones

- ♦ Lining of the lip aperture and the (flute's) embouchure hole
- ♦ Size and shape of the lip aperture
- ♦ Proper posture, breathing and breath support

Hooting and Luring of the Sound

- ♦ A mental image of hooting into a barrel with an open and light sound
- ♦ A precise and focused airstream and a clear onset
- ♦ Your sides open up with small breaths between the notes

a)

Bouncing

- ◆ Air staccato (*huh-huh*, without tonguing)
- ◆ A light bounce from the abs and sufficient air speed
- ◆ Totally free airstream and no obstructions

b)

Easy Warm-ups with Scales

Transpose the exercises into different keys, including the relative minor keys. You can easily transpose the exercises by using any scale book you have available or by writing the exercises down on the blank staff at the end of the book. Try also transposing them by ear.

a) Legato

b) Air staccato (*Huh-huh*, without tonguing)

c) Air + tongue reflex (*hü-dü*)

d) Staccato

Simile

a) Legato

b) Air staccato

c)   Air + tongue reflex

d)   Staccato

Simile

a)   Legato

b)   Air staccato

c)   Air + tongue reflex

d)   Staccato

Whole Scale

a) Legato

b) Air staccato

c) Air + tongue reflex

d) Staccato

Frame the Flute with Fingers for Stability

- Use the following fingerings to balance and stabilize the flute:
  - LH Thumb, middle finger, little finger
  - RH Thumb, index finger, little finger
- Close the keys (don't press!) and feel the balance. Then play
  normally keeping the flute totally still and fingers close
  to the keys.

Bicycle Pump

- ♦ Keep the air moving with an impression of a bicycle pump.
- ♦ Check that the sound is pure and free from unwanted noise.
- ♦ Add a light bounce from the abs (*hi-ah, hi-ah*).

a)

b)

c)

Simile in Different Keys

a)

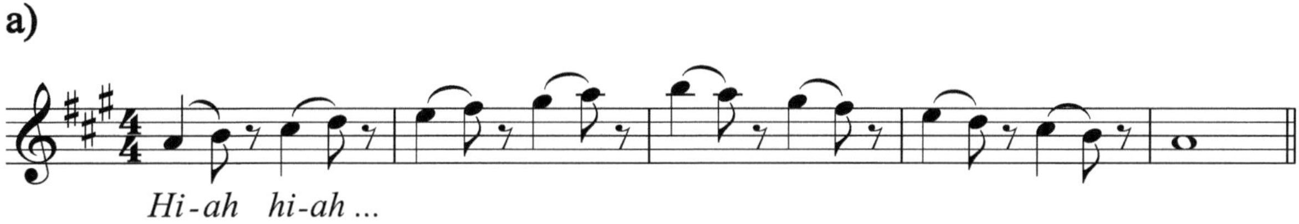

b)

c)

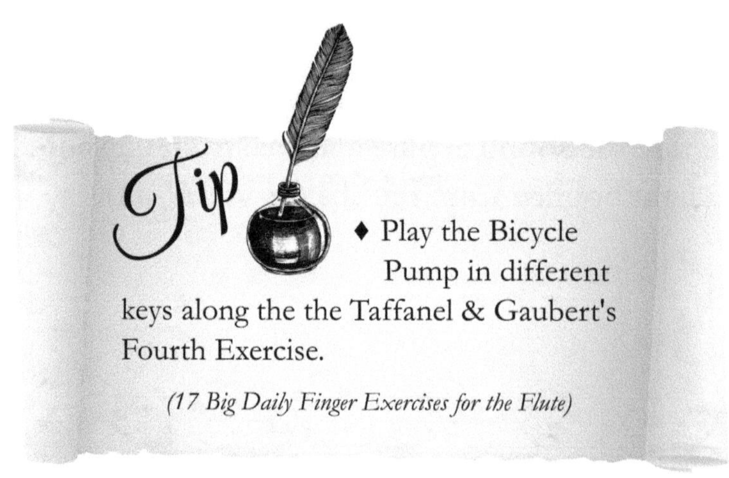

Bright Staccatos

- ♦ Play with relaxed and open sound on a solid ground.
- ♦ Let the air supplies fill up automatically between the notes.
- ♦ Keep the air moving.

a) Air staccato (play without tongue)

b)

c) Add tonguing that's reflex-like and quick as a lizard.

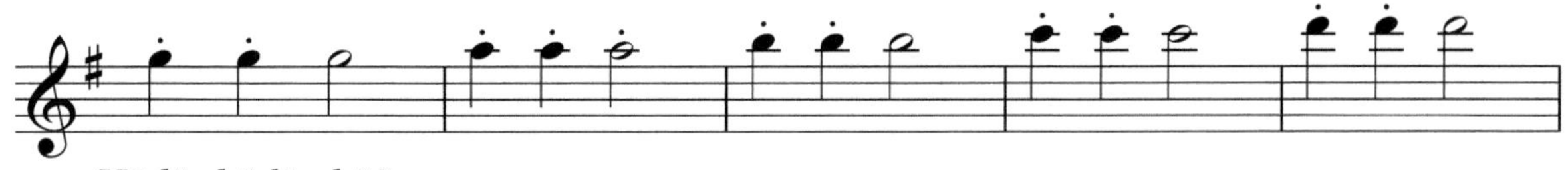

d)

e)

Quick Breaths

- ♦ Use air staccatos or play the note with the help of the consonant /p/.
- ♦ Try reflex-like staccatos: fill up the air supply between the staccatos quickly.

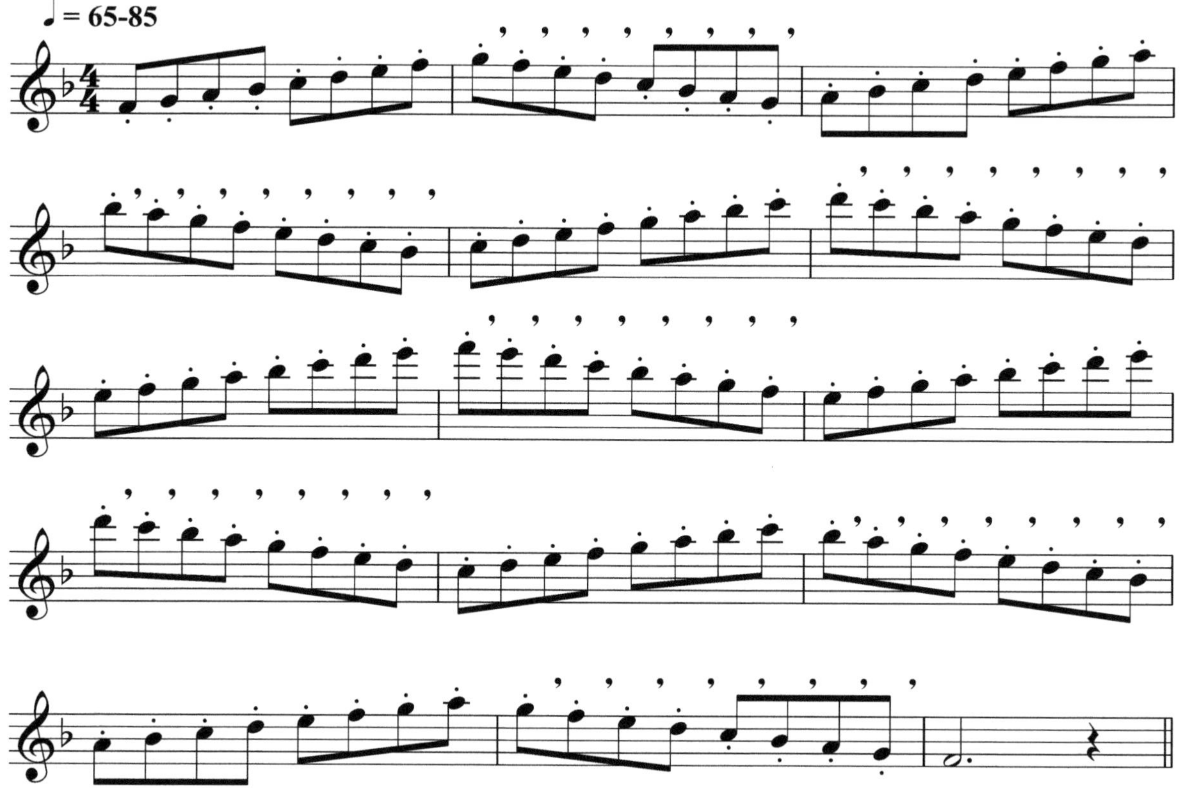

- ♦ Check that the tone doesn't crack in the middle register.

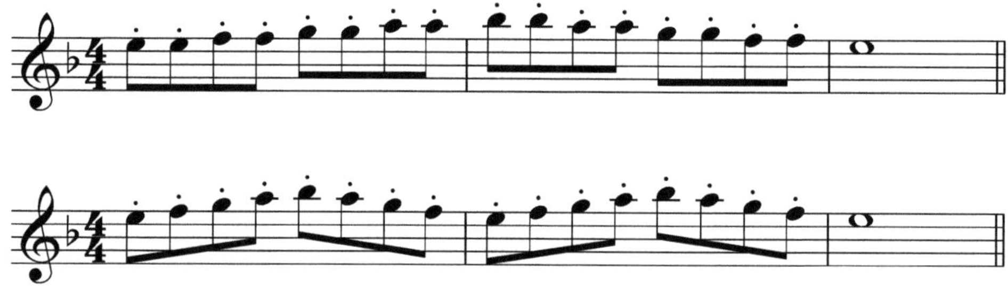

Play in different keys. (Taffanel & Gaubert's Fourth Exercise)

Vowels and Tone Colors

Different timbres and tone colors can be found by changing the shape and size of the oral cavity with the help of the tongue and pharynx. Test different vowels that appear in your native language and other languages you know. Try different combinations of the vowels according to what feels natural. You will learn to adjust the shape and size of the oral cavity to fit different registers. Make use of vowels also when adjusting intonation.

/æ/ - the vowel as in the word 'sad'
/ɜ/ - the vowel in the word 'purr'
/ɔ:/ - the vowel in the word 'door'
/ɑ:/ - the vowel in the word 'car'
/e/ - the vowel in the word 'sell'
/u:/ - the vowel in the word 'pew'

a)   Add vowels to the blow:

b)   Think of two things at the same time: the feeling of forming an *ü* with the lips and a sense of bigger vowels inside the mouth.

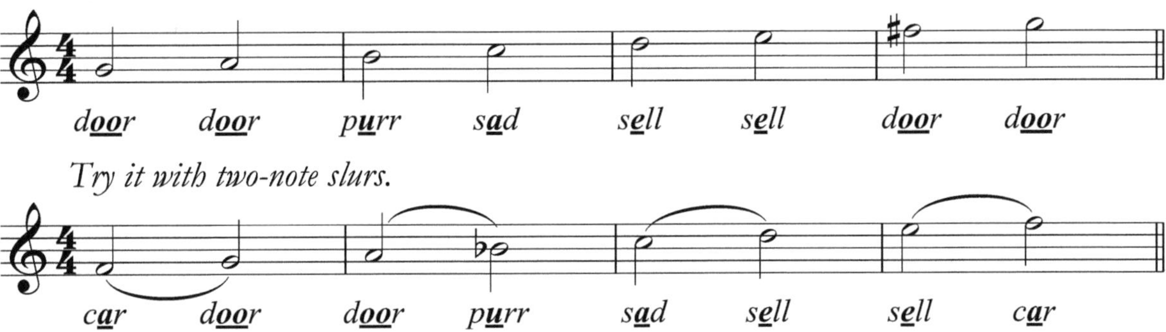

c)   Try it with the chromatic scale.

In faster passages, think about vowels mainly at the beginning and at the end of the phrase.

Chromatic Vowel Warm-up

♦ Slide from one note to another as smoothly as possible. Imagine stretching a rubber band gently.

Playing and Singing

This exercise helps you to improve the sound quality and to find a relaxed
position for the larynx.

- ♦ Learn to switch the vibration of vocal cords on and off.
- ♦ Maintain the same resonance in the playing as you would when singing.
- ♦ Sing smoothly and gently and find a key that fits your vocal range.
- ♦ Sing and play easy, short phrases.

a) Preparation. First, sing a relaxed *"ah"* /ɑ:/ (the vowel in the word 'car'),
    with the flute in the playing position. Bring your lips closer to a normal
    embouchure and smoothly transition to sing and play simultaneously.

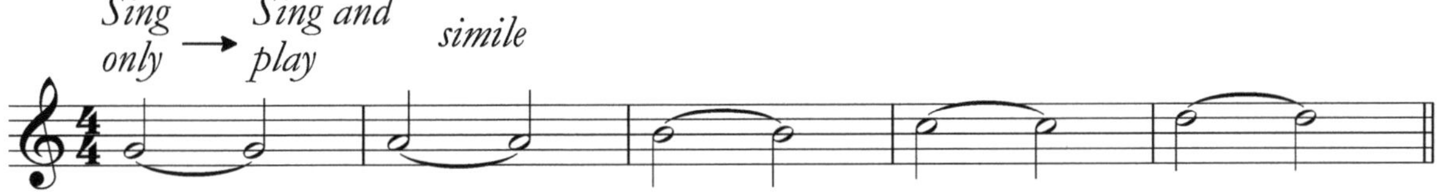

b)

Brother John / Frère Jacques (French Nursery Rhyme)

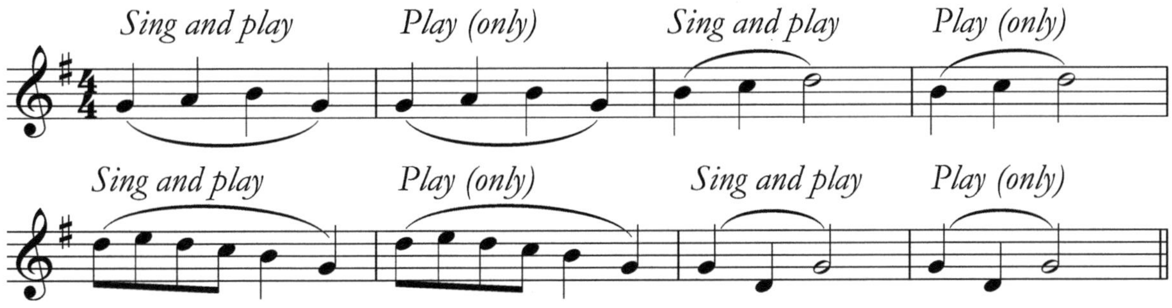

Relaxing Flutter Tonguing Exercises

Flutter tonguing will help you to produce an even airstream and to relax your throat.

- ♦ First let out a relaxed sigh of relief.
- ♦ Then play a note with the same feeling of relief and let the tip of the tongue flutter on top of the airstream.
- ♦ Relax the jaw. Check that you don't clench your teeth.

a) From middle C to low G

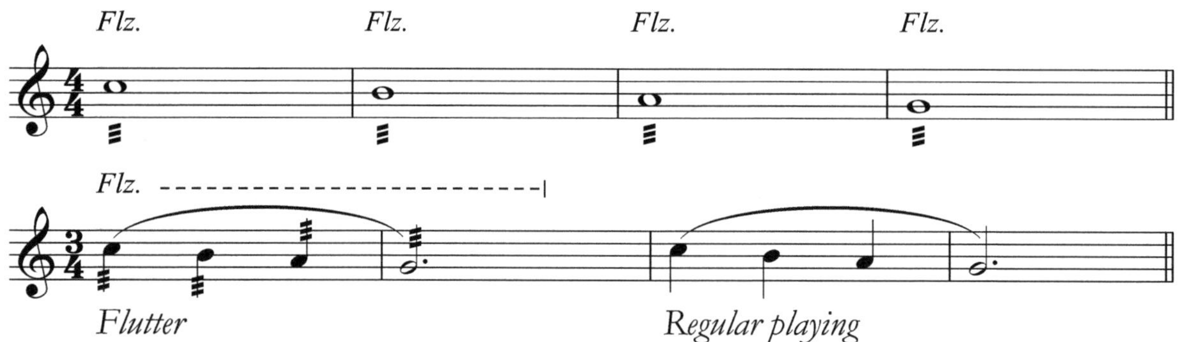

b) From middle D to middle G

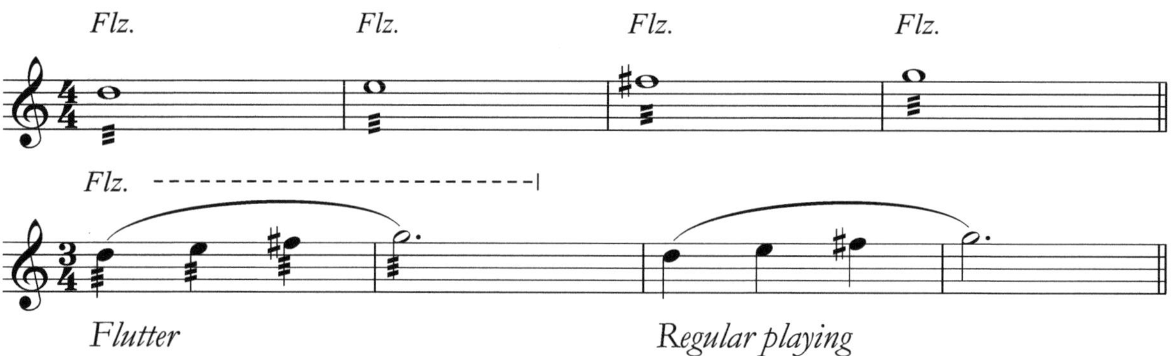

c) The whole scale

d) Chromatically from middle C to low E

e) Chromatically from middle C to high C

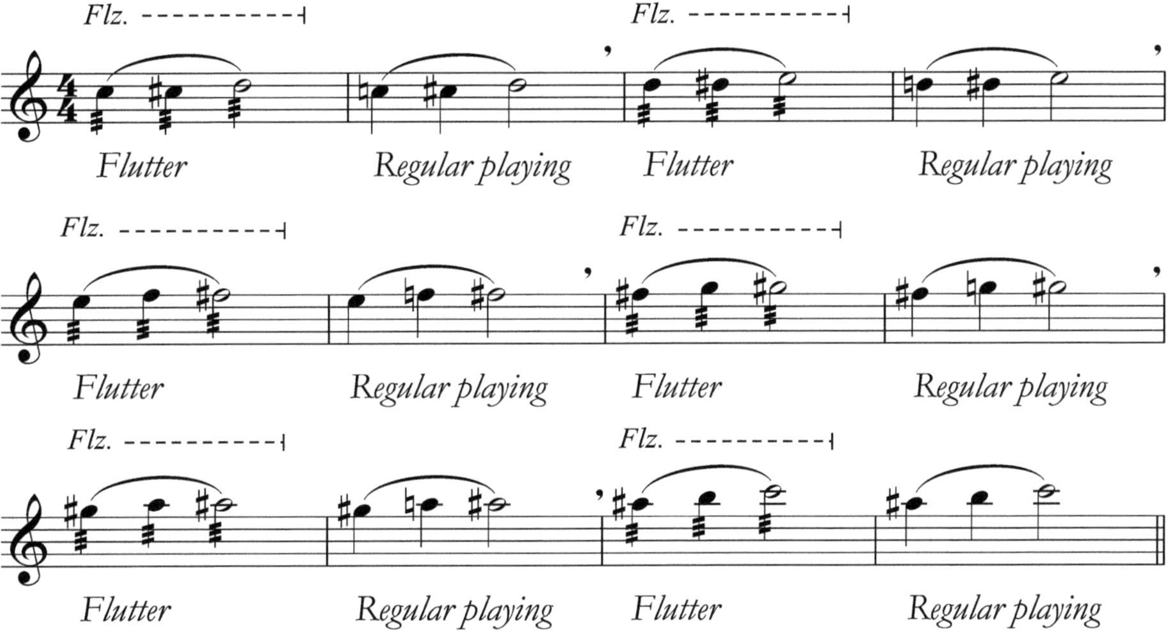

Brother John / Frère Jacques (French Nursery Rhyme)

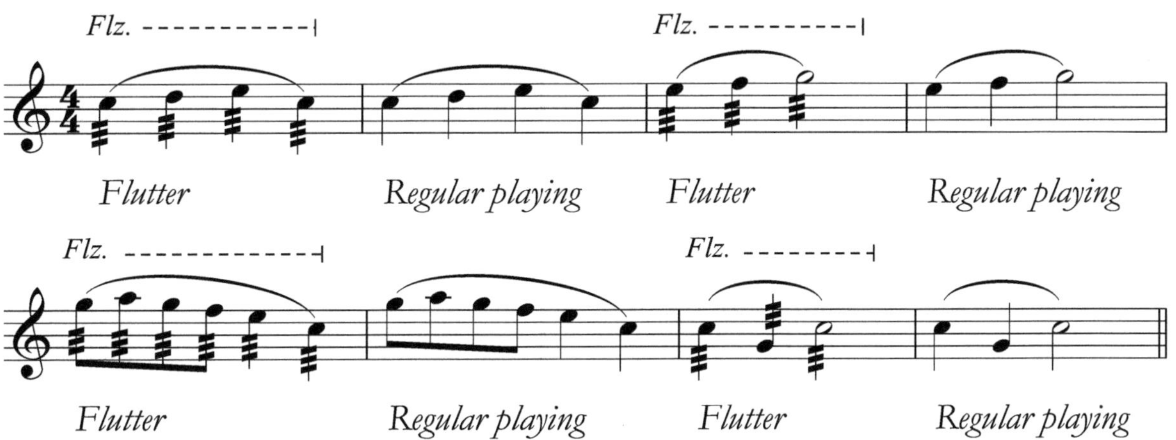

3

Quality of Sound

Basics

Practice the correct breathing technique first. Then learn how to save air and not to overblow. For the correct pitch and intonation adjustment, air needs a sufficient amount of air pressure and it should be quick and focused. Don't push the air out with the neck muscles. Use your lower abdominal muscles for supporting the air. At the same time, the intercostal muscles should prevent your ribcage from collapsing while playing.

When the sound has a good focus, no air gets wasted. Air can be projected into different cavities so that the sound resonates in different parts of the body, as in singing. When you sing or play a note you see on the staff, the fundamental note resonates in the body as well as other frequencies of the harmonic series. Imagine that the airstream starts from the legs and swirls through the body all the way to the resonance spot between your eyes and out through the lip aperture. This image will help you to add brightness, freedom and resonance to the sound.

If the flute wobbles when you play, it breaks the focus and evenness of the blow. If the finger movements are too heavy or the flute rests too loosely on the chin, it will be difficult to keep the flute stable.

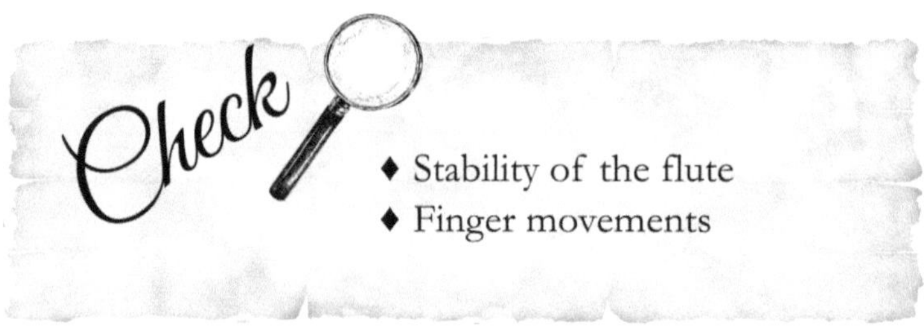

Glowing Sound

- ♦ Aim for an easy, bright and beautiful B natural.
- ♦ Play with your eyes closed and imagine you are singing.
- ♦ Copy the tone color and resonance of the previous tone.
- ♦ While descending, don't lose the tone quality and the resonance.

Preparation

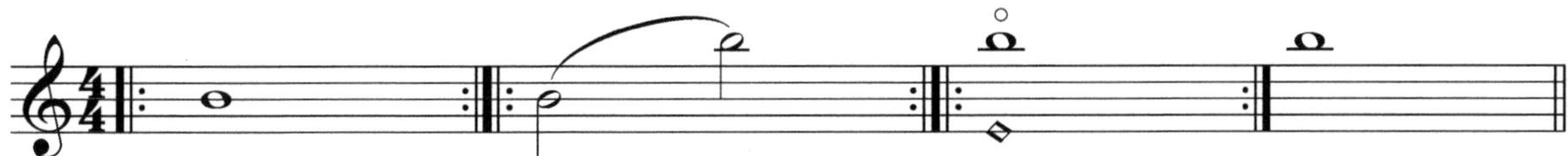

a) From middle B to low C

b) The same idea with three slurred notes from middle B to low C

c)

$\mathcal{T}\!est\ it$

How to prevent the air from escaping too fast?

♦ Imagine there is an air cushion in your belly. When you blow, the cushion should stay down and remain puffy and beautiful.

♦ Imagine you have small air tanks between your ribs. Air is precious so be careful not to let it out too fast. This image prevents the sides from collapsing and helps you to retain internal air pressure when you blow.

Butterfly Wings

- ♦ Again, aim to maintain the same tone quality and brightness.
- ♦ The fingers move lightly but precisely like butterfly wings.
- ♦ Move the fingers from the first knuckle.
- ♦ Play in different keys.

a)

You can also cut the bars in half and play a shorter version.

Flageolets as Reference Tones

You can use flageolets (*see p. 48*) as reference tones by alternating between flageolet – standard fingering - flageolet – standard fingering.

(Play high notes with the low register fingerings.)

♦ Slur with two notes.
♦ Imagine a glowing butterfly descending.

b)

♦ Imagine searching
for the right path
in a dark forest with
a headlamp. When you play the long tone,
you find the way into the light.

- ♦ Slur with three notes ascending.
- ♦ Use different vowels *(door, car, sell, car)*.

c)

◆ Slur with three notes descending.

◆ Search for a bright spot, check that the tones are not flat and dull.

d)

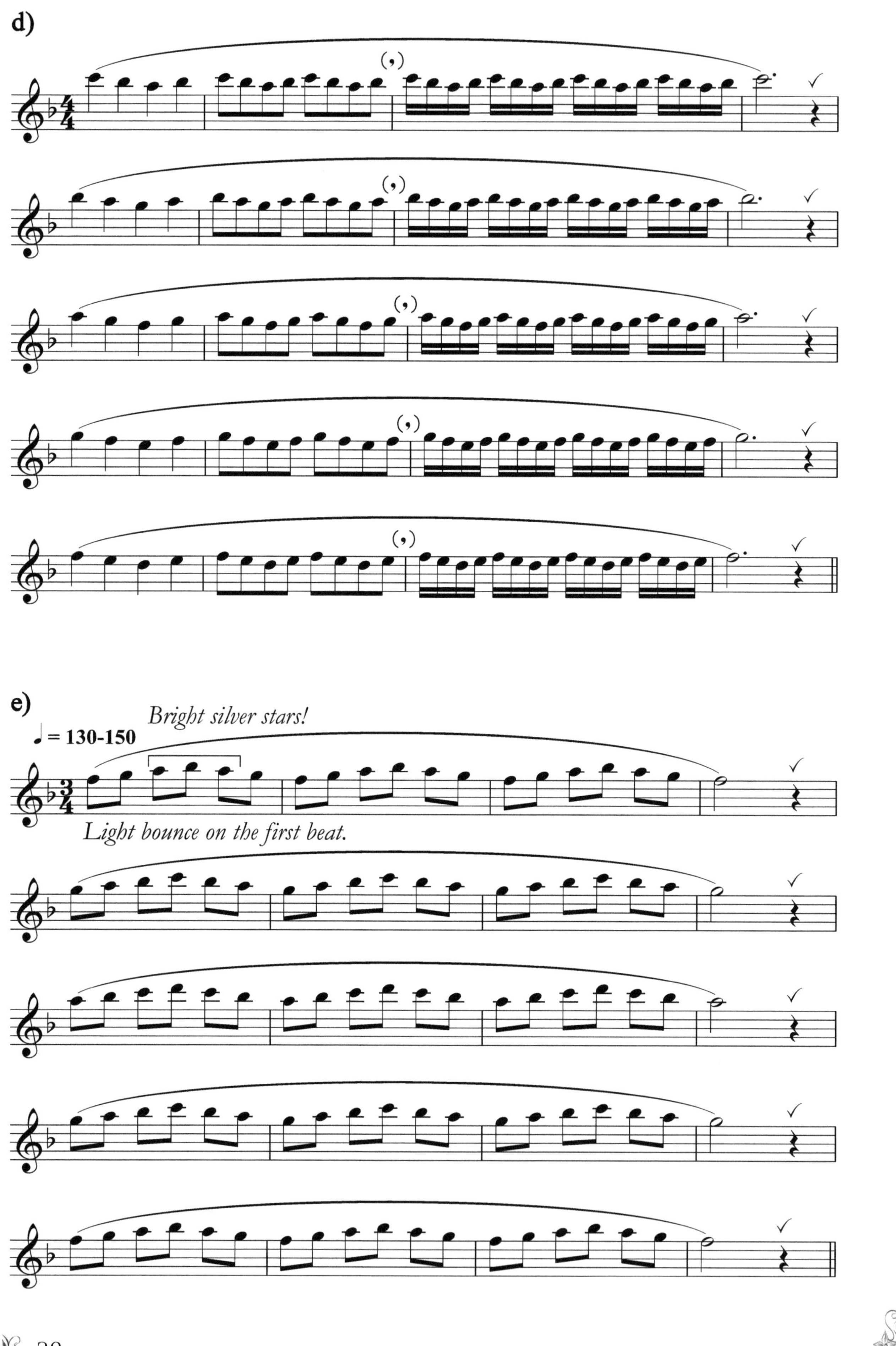

e)

Flowing Swan

- ◆ **Maintain high sound quality while descending.**
- ◆ **Try different tone colors** (*see p. 51*).

a)

b)

- ◆ Play in a sensitive manner in *ppp*, i.e. as quietly and delicately as you can.
- ◆ Check the intonation of the lower notes from the tuning meter.

c)

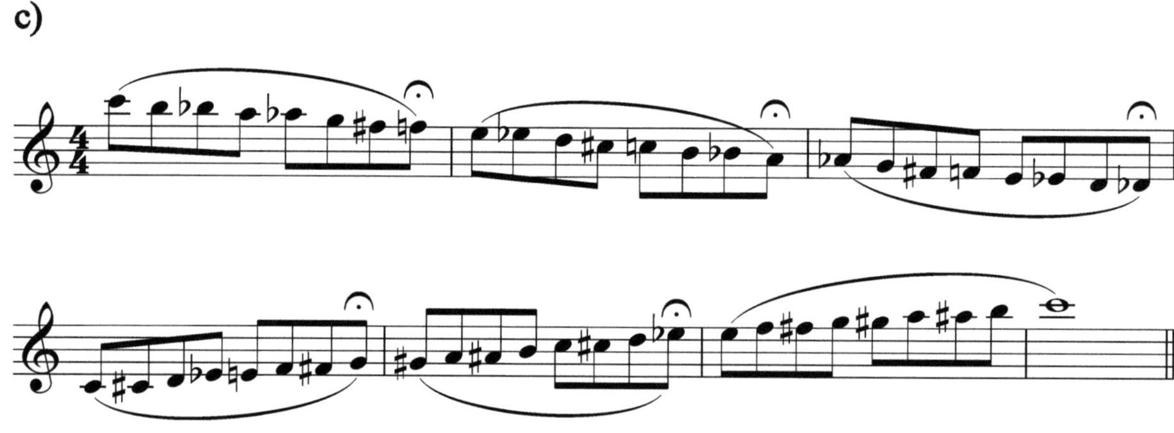

Tremolos

Play in a flexible and relaxed manner.

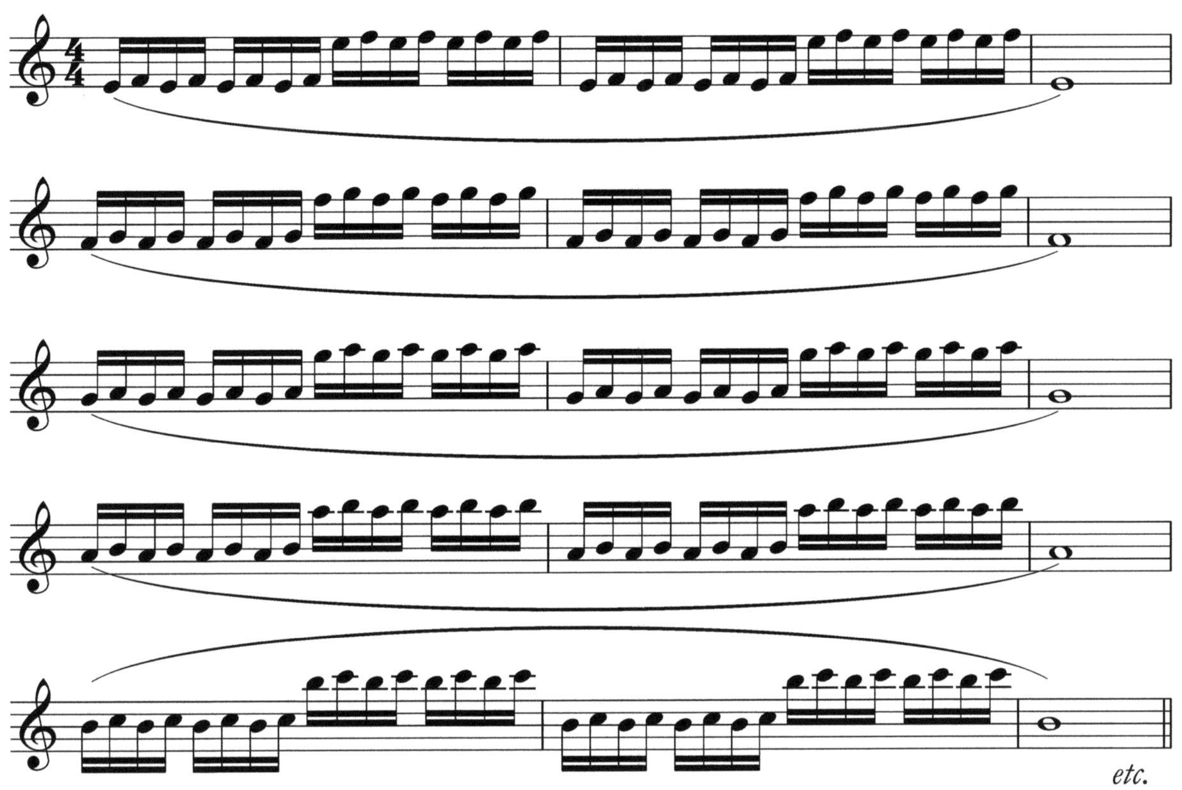

etc.

Octave and Tone Exercises

Octaves as Reflexes

- ♦ Play without the tongue.
- ♦ Play like a diver bird calling at the lake *(koh - klew 'ee)*.
- ♦ Keep the octave leaps fast and reflex-like.
- ♦ On the leap think the corners of the mouth a bit forward.
- ♦ Play the long tones brightly and clearly.
- ♦ Play juicy and fleshy low notes.

a)

- ♦ Do the same thing from the top downwards.
- ♦ Now start with the tongue. Keep the ends of the slurs light.
- ♦ Sing in your mind e.g., *Dee-ah dee-ah dee-aah!*

b)

Mountain Climbing

♦ Play without the tongue *(Huh-huh-hooo)*.
♦ Use a sufficient amount of air.

a)

- ♦ Play simile from low D to high D.
- ♦ Low notes can be round and fleshy.
- ♦ Play the long tone freely and openly.
- ♦ Check that you don't force the sound or turn the flute inward.

b)

- ♦ Play simile from high D to low D.
- ♦ Think about climbing down from a mountain with steady steps.

c)

Super Legato

- ♦ Find the easiest spot for both registers.
- ♦ Experiment with a violin-like legato and the use of a bow.

a)

◆ Play the octave leaps as smoothly as possible without gaps between the notes *("super-legato")*.

b)

◆ Try the same idea faster.
◆ Again, imagine having a violinist or cellist's bow.
◆ Find the easiest way and check that you don't force the sound.

c)

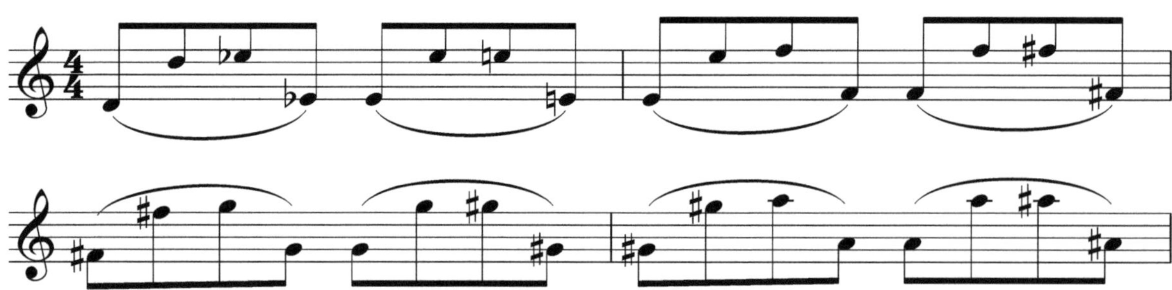

Flageolets

Overblown harmonics known as flageolets can be used as reference tones. Play the note as a flageolet first and then with the same feel using standard fingering. By practicing flageolets you will find an optimal embouchure for different registers. Flageolets can be played with the same fingering, by alternating the pressure of the blow. In practice, overblowing means simply speeding up the air flow, adjusting air pressure and the size of the lip aperture. This way it is possible to play the upper register softly.

> ♦ Play without the tongue and avoid pinching.
> ♦ Keep the chin, neck area and root of the tongue relaxed.
> ♦ Do not focus too much on the intonation; flageolets will be flat.

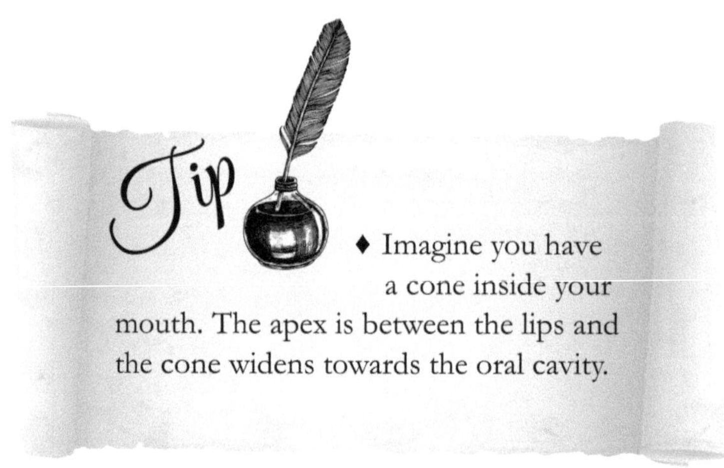

a) Play an octave and a fifth with a low register fingerings. Look for the best and easiest spot for every note.

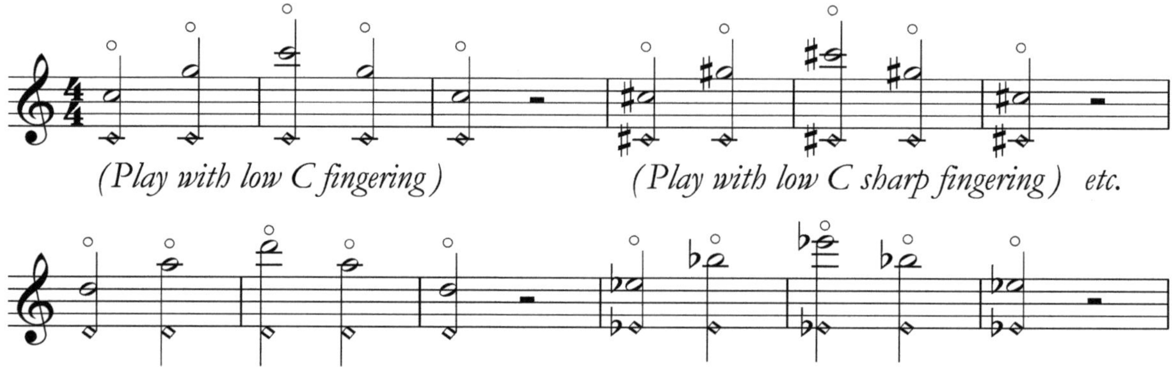

b) Legato

c) Scale trick!

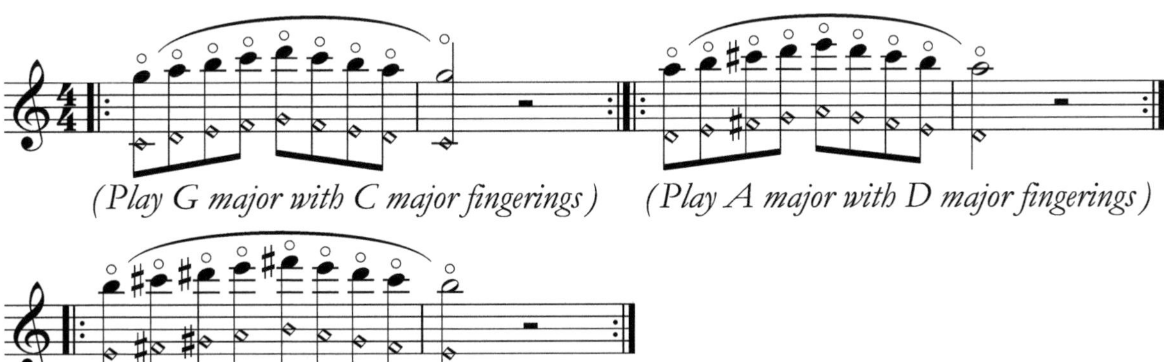

d) Another scale trick!

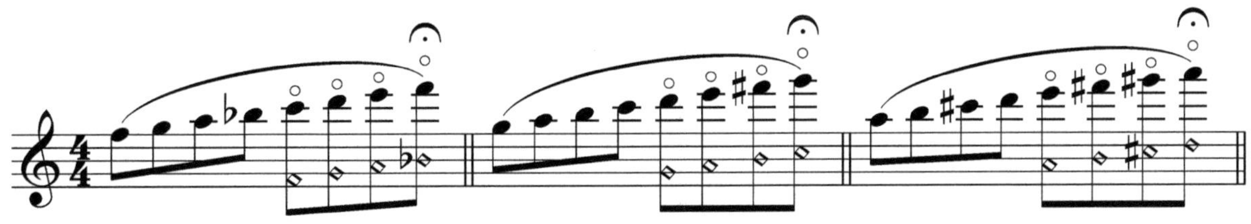

Harmonics:

Fog Horn Sounds

With this exercise, you learn to add harmonics, resonance and depth to the sound.

1. Regular fingering
2. Use an upper register fingering
3. Back to regular fingering

1. Play the first note lightly and sweetly *(mp)*.

2. Let the ghost note (the same note with upper register fingering) grow, like a ship's fog horn. Imagine playing the tones from behind a mask.

3. Then go back to regular fingering, but now with an even deeper and richer tone.

Tone Color and Finger Exercises

From Light to Dark

Finnish flutist and flute pedagogue Tapio Jalas has identified the following two main tone colors:

Frame sound: Light, booming and hollow, a wooden flute sound
Centered sound: Dark, compact, nasal, oboe-like sound

- ◆ Explore tone colors with one note. Play gradually from a light to dark tone.
- ◆ Different tone colors can be found with small adjustments.

- Light tone: *cute, cotton wool, aquarelle* etc.
- Dark tone: *an evil witch, compact foil ball, a diamond drill* etc.
- Find your favourite tone color which includes both.

Triplets à la Moyse

The aim is to find a balanced tone color.

- First play the phrase with one tone, then change the color.
- Keep the triplet fingerings light and exact, don't squeeze the instrument.
- Try an impression of fluttering butterfly wings.
- Check that the flute is stable.

1. Use a light frame sound.
2. Use a dark centered sound.

a)

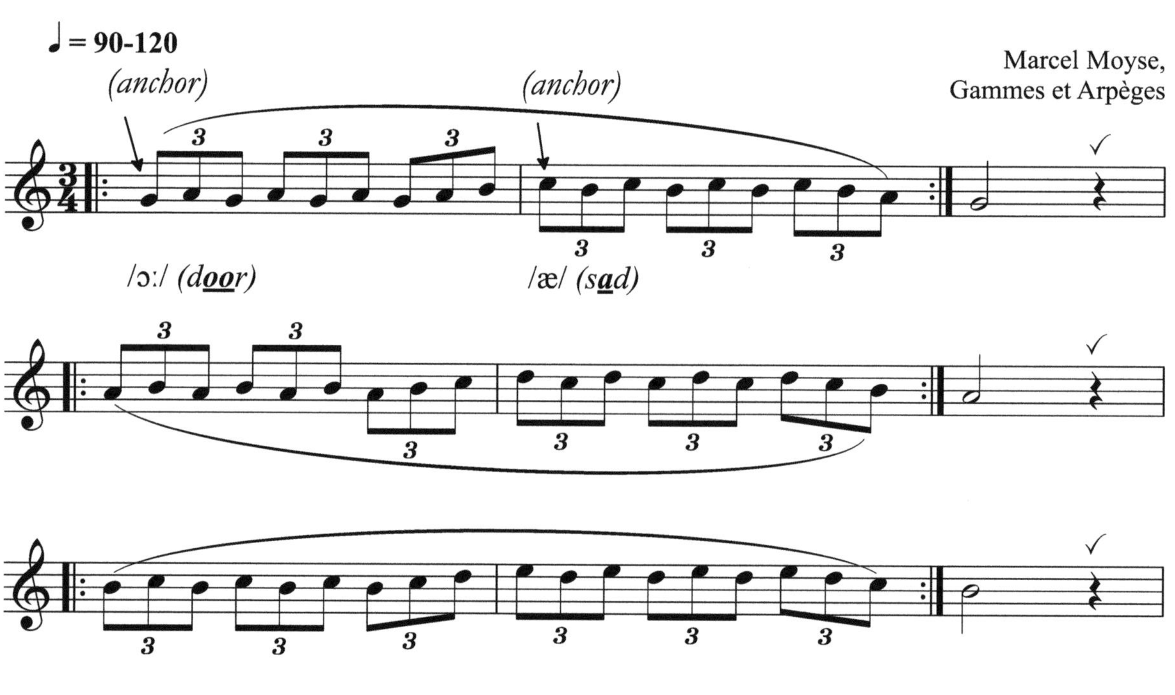

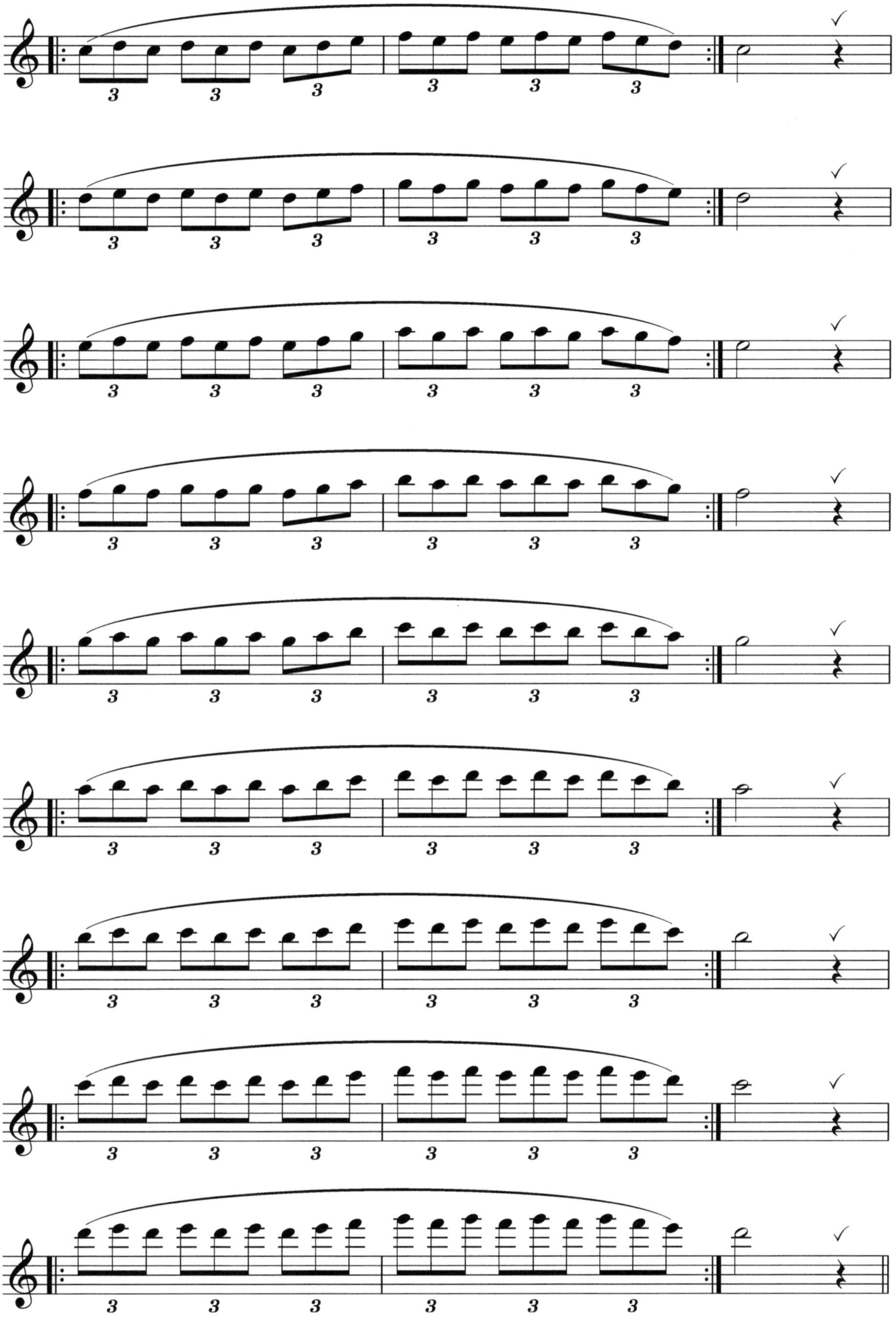

3. Use both colors.

b) Alternate between different tone colors and nuances during the same phrase.

From a wooden flute sound to an an oboe-like sound...

From an oboe-like sound to a wooden flute sound...

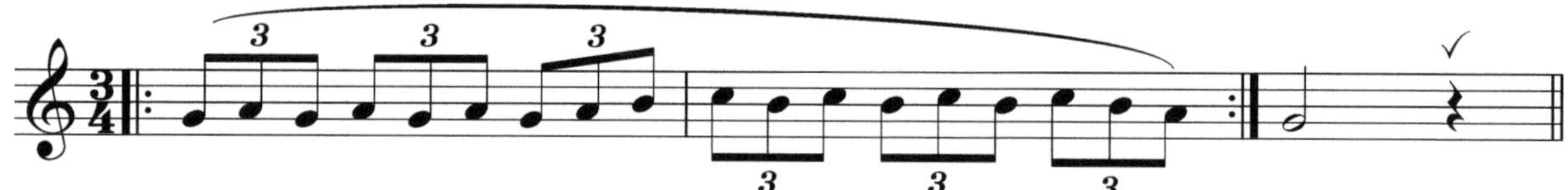

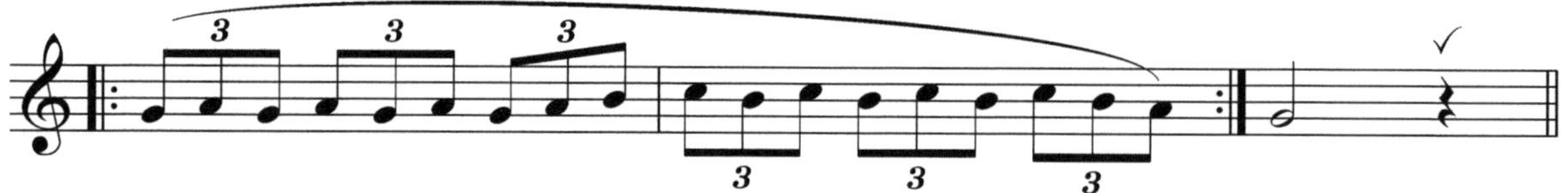

Triplets with Chromatics

a) Chromatic variation of Marcel Moyse's exercise

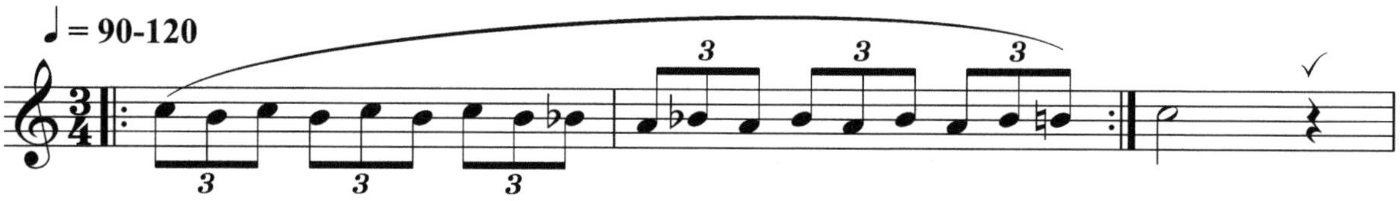

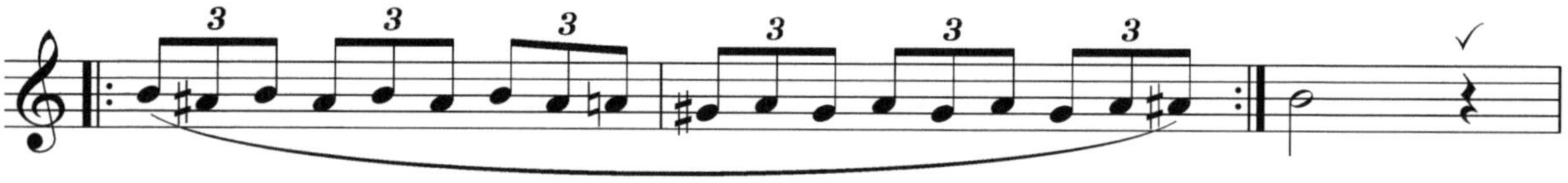

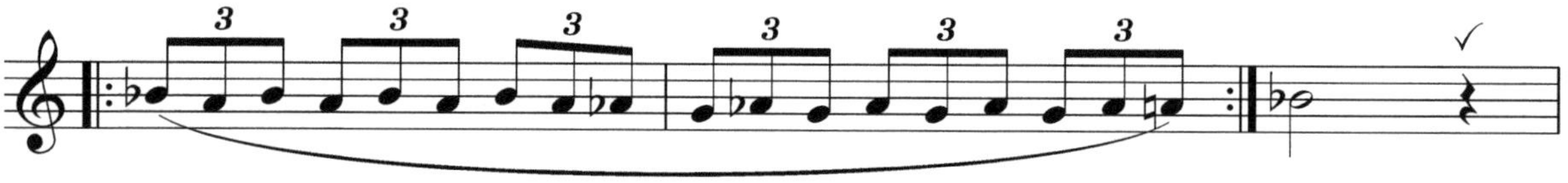

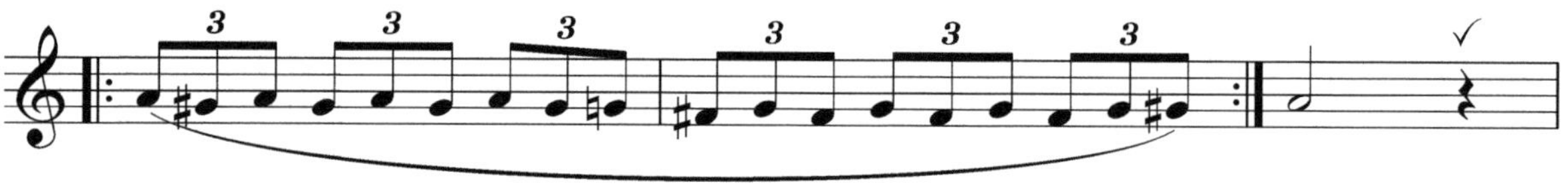

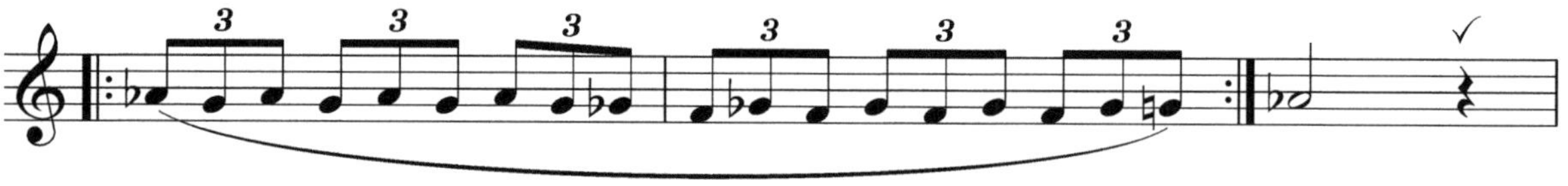

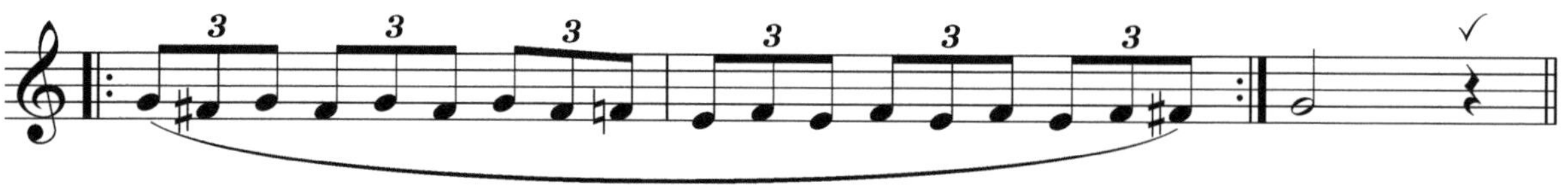

b) Ascending with triplets

c)

Pointers for Hands, Fingers and Stability

Too much muscle effort when holding the flute will create the sensation that the flute is heavier than it actually is. Remember to take small breaks between practice sessions and shake off your hands and arms properly to get rid of the tension.

The carpal tunnels pass through the wrists. To prevent hand problems and strain injuries it is important not to squeeze the wrist bones. Try softening and loosening your wrists while playing. Lift your fingers from the first knuckle and stay close to the keys. There is no need to press the keys, it will only slow your fingers down. Use a minimum effort to open and close the keys.

Quick Chromatic Runs

♦ With a light, bouncy and cute sound
♦ Active and precise fingers, reflex-like grace notes
♦ Preparing the next quick notes during the break

a) Grace notes

b)   One triplet upwards

One triplet downwards

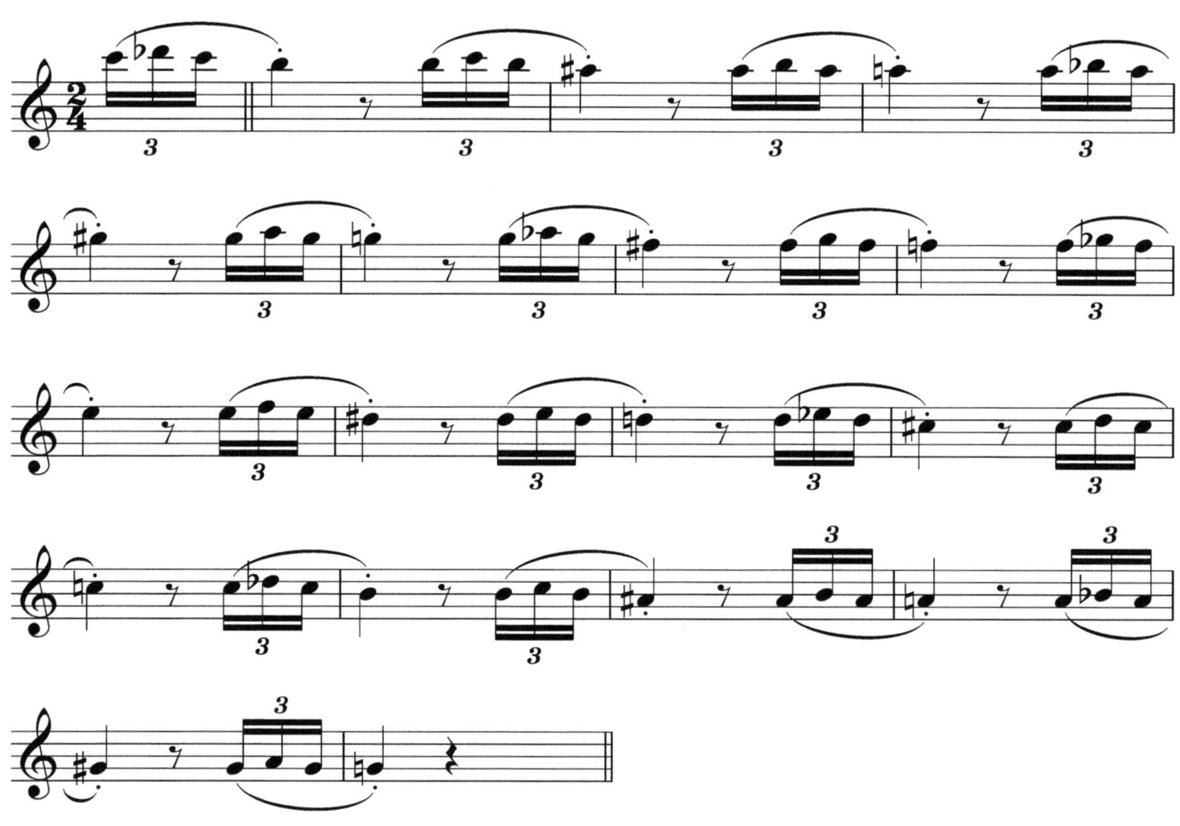

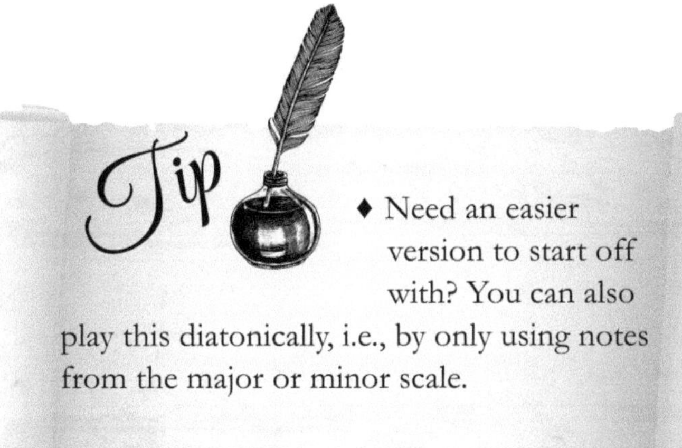

c) Two triplets upwards. During the rest prepare for the next pattern.

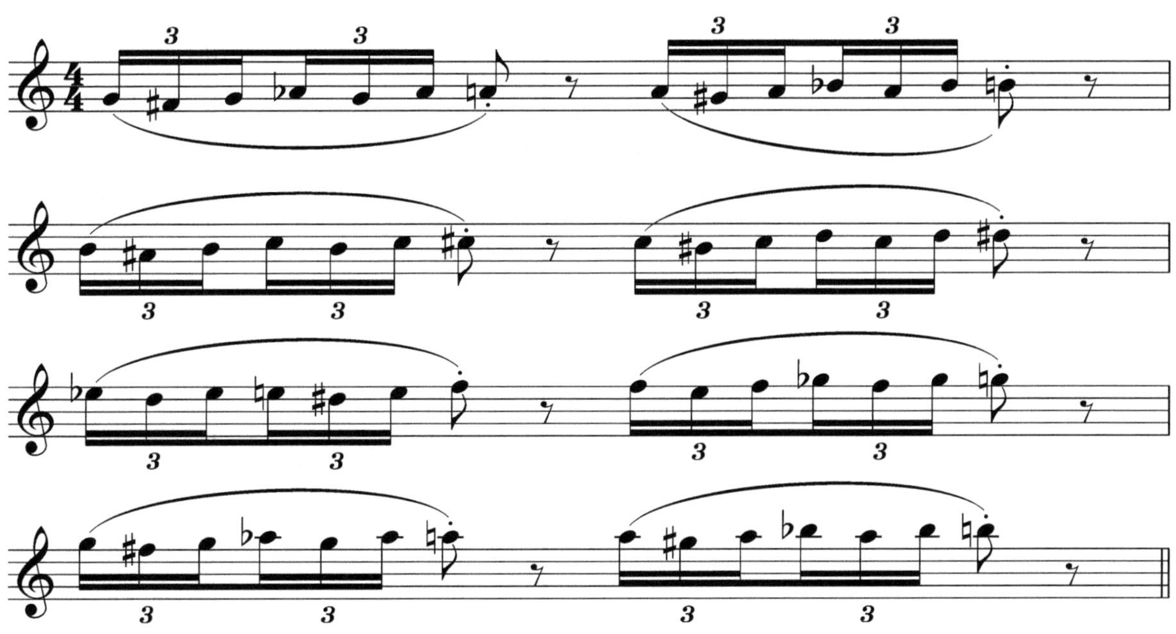

Two triplets downwards

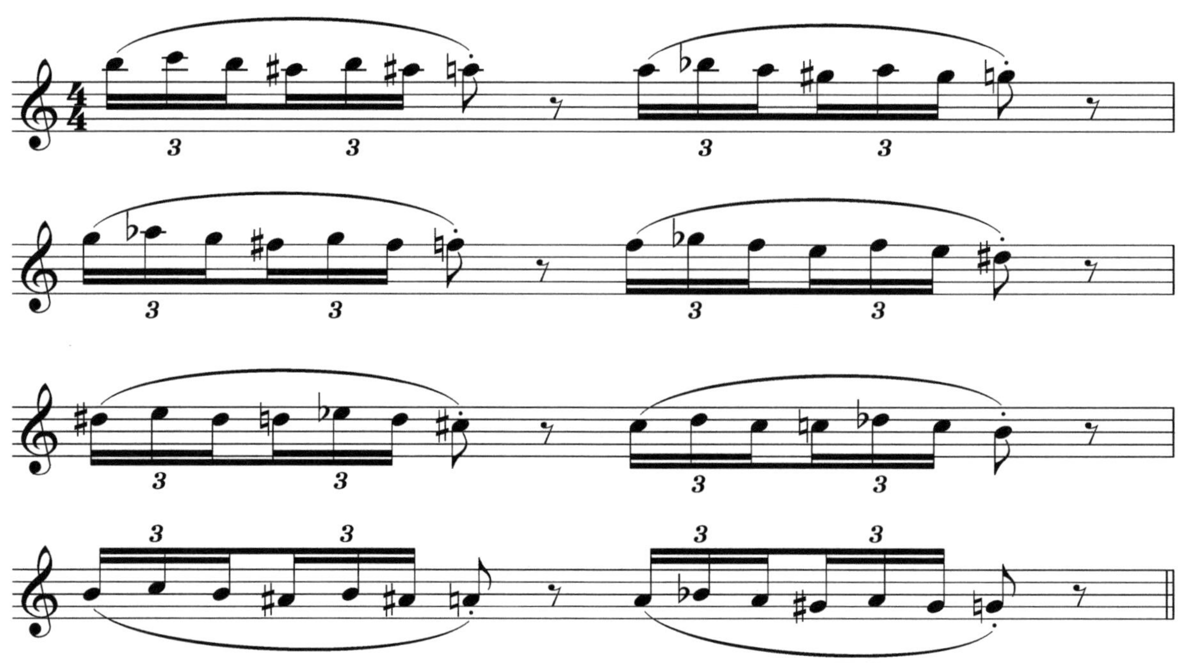

Triplet Chains

a)

b) Simile with a different rhythm

- ♦ Play with a round and light sound.
- ♦ Alternate between different articulations.

c) Triplet game in low register

Articulation 2 + 1

Articulation 1 + 2

d) Simile with double tonguing

Practice Tips for Fast Patterns

a) Play SLOWLY with a high-quality tone.

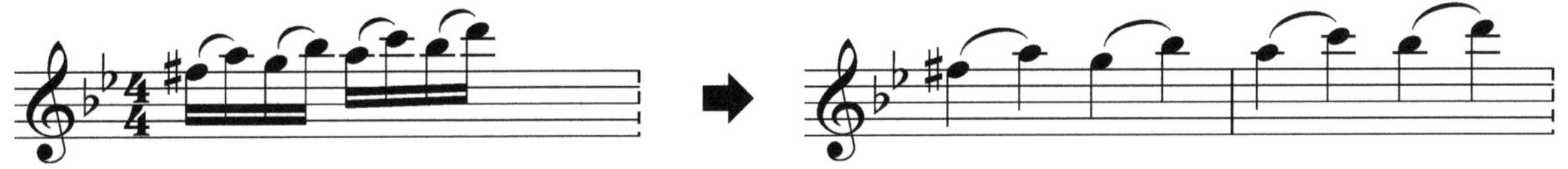

b) Spot the most challenging fingerings. Repeat them three times in a row.

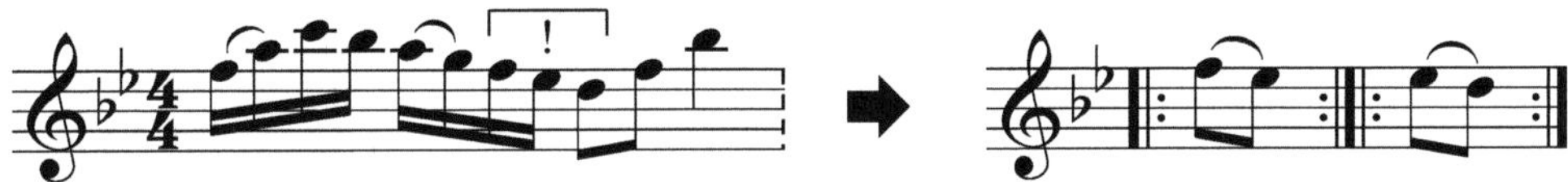

c) Play two notes quickly and slurred. Pause.
Think of the next pattern during the pause.

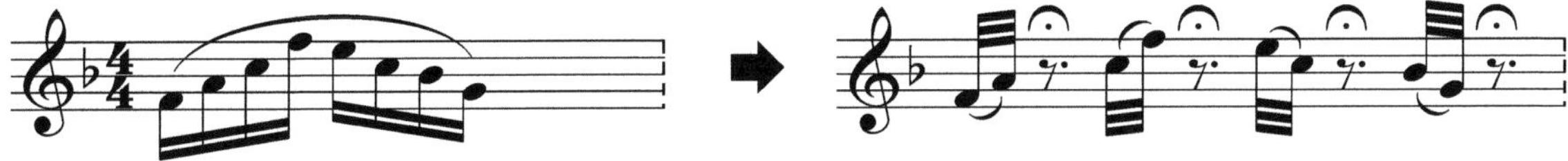

Play four notes quickly and slurred. Pause. Go on.

d) Play 4 +1 pattern. Play rhythmic variations.

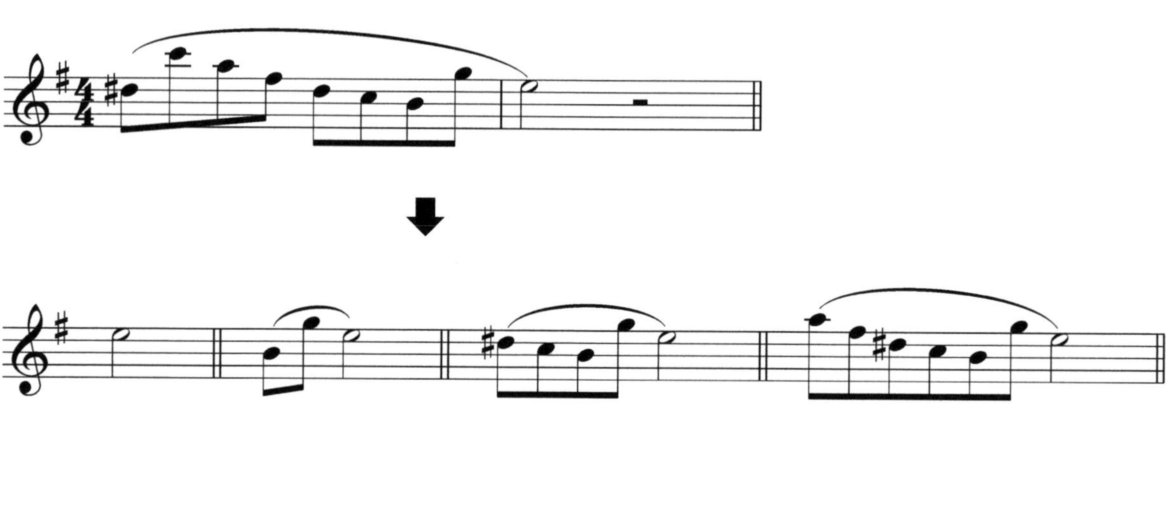

e) Play the pattern starting form the last note. Unfold it one by one.

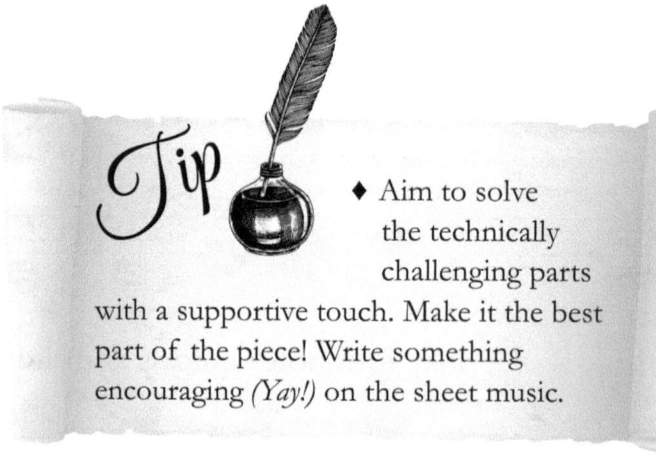

4

Thoughts on Breathing and Posture

Breathing

Breathing exercises tend to work best with simple images and visualization. It is important that breathing feels natural to you. Natural positions of the body, where breathing happens in its natural place can be very useful. You can also activate deep breathing with different images, for example, imagining that you direct the air into the back pockets of your jeans can help to deepen the breath.

Deep breathing supports your playing. It makes your belly, back and ribs expand. Breathing begins from your diaphragm and from the relaxation of your abdomen and throat. In addition to different ways of breathing, it's useful to think of the places where you inhale the air. You can also locate good spots for breathing by singing your phrases.

Observe and listen to your own way of breathing. When we are stressed out and tense, our breathing becomes faster and shallower. During shallow breathing, the use of the diaphragm is ineffective and consequently your sound is more tense. Also, you must learn how to breathe quickly and unnoticeably between the phrases. During quick breathing, tension is released and your lungs suck the air in. Breathing happens as if by itself, as a reflex.

Test it

♦ Raise your chest a little so that you get a bit more space for your abdomen. A slightly raised chest enables you to breathe automatically more effortlessly.

♦ Don't let your chest or ribs collapse during the phrase. Imagine that your chest is a cupboard. Keep the doors open!

Movement Directions Associated to Diaphragmatic Breathing

(Lea Pearson: Body Mapping for Flutists 2006)

Inhalation

- The diaphragm moves downwards
- The abdominal wall moves outwards
- The ribs move outwards and upwards
- The back moves outwards
- The pelvic floor moves downwards

Exhalation

- The diaphragm returns to its original place, i.e., moves upwards
- The pelvic floor returns upwards
- The abdominal area moves inwards
- The ribs move down and inwards

Check Certain types of breathing can be harmful for you. Make sure you don't do too much of the following:

Clavicular Breathing

- Superficial breathing, shoulders rise
- Fills only the upper parts of the lungs

Chest Breathing

- Chest gasping for air
- The abdomen is tense
- Insufficient usage of the diaphragm
- The back doesn't open enough

Superficial Belly Breathing

- The belly expands considerably
- The ribs and the back don't open sufficiently

Breathing Exercises

Scent of Flowers

Breathe in slowly through the nose *(hmmm)* and imagine smelling a flower. Feel a beginning of a yawn in your throat. Let out a big sigh *(aaaaah…)*. It's the same relaxed feeling as when you come home after a long day and lift your feet up.

Flying Flutist

Raise your arms up slowly and smoothly, inhaling at the same time. Lower your arms when you exhale, through a small slit between the lips. Repeat. Count for example 1-2-3-4 (inhale) 1-2-3-4-5-6-7-8 (exhale).

Release of the Upper Body

Sit on the edge of a chair and bend your upper body over and let it hang loosely. Your head, neck and arms are hanging totally relaxed, your chest is resting on your knees. In this position, observe the movement of your breath in your torso and especially in your back.

Automatic Fill

Blow out all your air slowly *(hssss…)*. At the end of the blow, wait for a couple of seconds. Then release and relax your abdomen and jaw. Inhalation happens by itself.

Pursed Lips

Breathe in and out through narrow, pursed lips. Take long breaths, slowly and smoothly. You can steer your breathing into different parts of your body.

Balanced Posture

A good posture is essential for healthy breathing when playing the flute. Use a mirror to check your side view posture. Is there a body part that is out of alignment? Are your knees locked? Notice especially the alignment of your pelvis and your head. Loosen your knee joints and let your tailbone drop down, imagine that you are a dinosaur with a massive tail.

Root your body into the ground and let it float up. The spine stretches out and upwards from the pelvis, long and tall thus freeing the upper torso. Your back feels long and wide. Your neck and head rise upwards, but the shoulders stay down. When your head is in a neutral position, the airflow is usually directed in a good angle.

CHECK THE ALIGNMENTS FOR BALANCED POSTURE:
ANKLES - KNEES - HIPS - SHOULDERS - HEAD

When seated, it's important that your pelvis doesn't tilt forward or backward:

Too much weight on the back part of your sitting bones		Upper torso collapses
Too much weight on the front part of the sitting bones	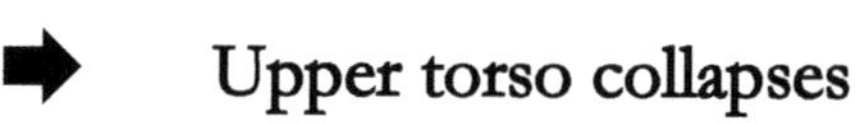	Tension in the back muscles

(Lea Pearson: *Body Mapping for Flutists* 2006)

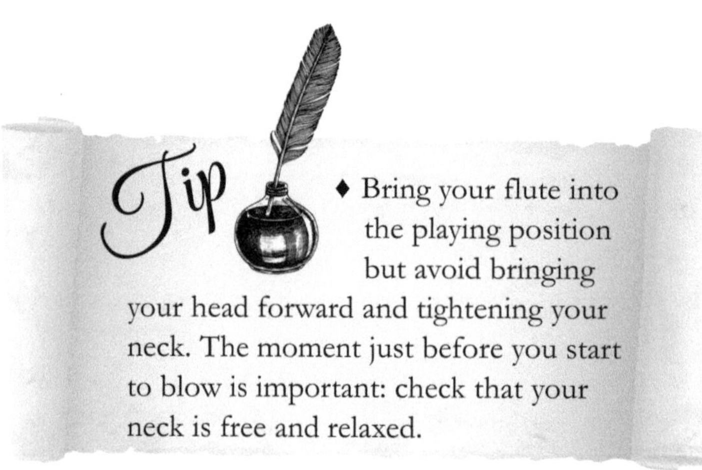

5

Tonguing

Basics

As a prerequisite for good sound, you need an airstream that supports tone. To get a clear onset, the tip of the tongue should be sufficiently in the front and close enough to the opening of the lips. If you hear a spitting sound, there is probably too much pressure behind the tongue. The attack should be clear and distinct. For example, the French syllables in such words as 'tu' and 'deux' are graceful and soft.

♦ Uninterrupted blow and only a tip
of the tongue surfs on top of air.
Hoo-doo-doo-doo-dooooo
♦ Try it with and without the flute.

Tonguing Exercises

Single Tongue Surfer

♦ Blow out a steady airstream and let the tongue surf on top of the
wave.
♦ Precise tonguing but only with the tip of the tongue.
♦ Keep the neck area relaxed.

a)

- ♦ Play up and down using major or minor scale.
- ♦ Practise in different keys.
- ♦ Keep steady airflow.

b)

- ♦ Play simile chromatically descending.
- ♦ Keep the articulation flexible and light.

c)

Peck Like a Bird with Flageolets

- ♦ Keep a sufficient air pressure, but don't squeeze the sound.
- ♦ Aim for an exact and clear attack.
- ♦ Imagine playing pizzicato on the violin (*d-d-d-d* etc.).

a)

Play at a faster tempo (d-d-d   d-d-d).
Think of quick and sharp pecking, like a woodpecker.
Tip of the tongue and abs in co-operation.

b)

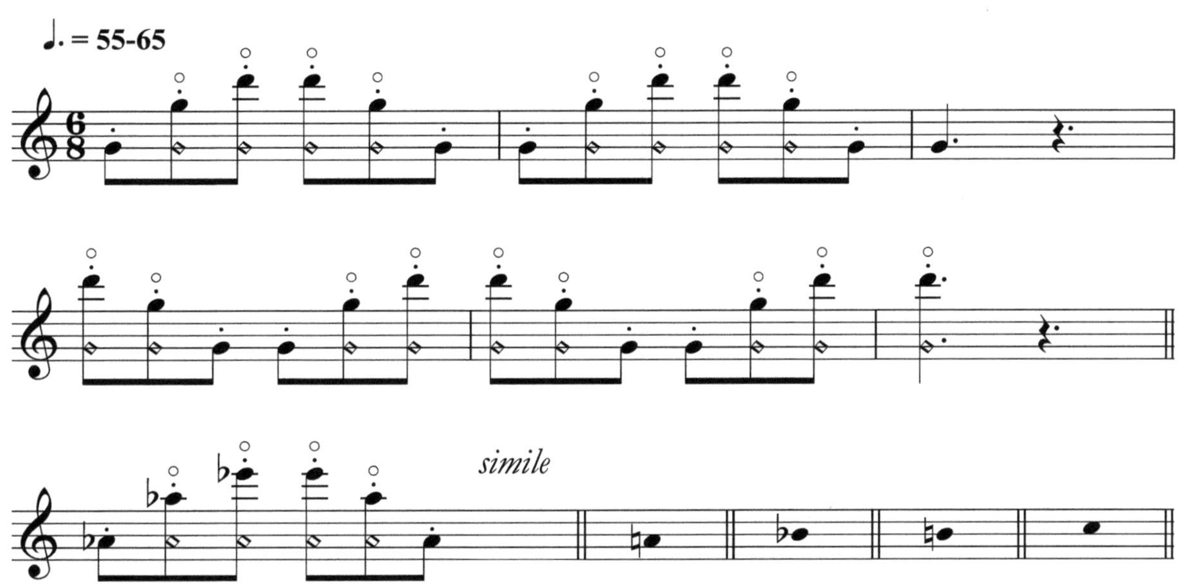

♩. = 55-65
simile

Pizzicato pecking descending chromatically
Tongue and fingers play exactly the same rhythm.

c)

♩ = 100-120
Simile descending cromatically.

Dotted Rhythm

- ◆ Sonorous swipe, like a violin bow.
- ◆ Keep the air moving and maintain the exact rhythm.
- ◆ Don't let the tongue disturb the sound.

a)

b) Dotted rhythm variation based on the Taffanel & Gaubert no 4.

First Variation

Swipe like a violin bow. Think of picking up the sixteenth notes.
Take quick breaths between notes.

Second Variation

Try a faster tempo. Play like a trumpet, more stable.

- ◆ Use different keys.
- ◆ Play quickly like a woodpecker.

c)

Simile in C major

Simile in G major

- ♦ Tip of the tongue acts like a guitar plectrum.
- ♦ Think of a delicate tap down, not a strike forward and back.
- ♦ Play chromatically and add one "pearl" into the chain of notes.

a) Two notes

b) Three notes

c) Four notes. In 3/4 time.

d) Five notes. Back to 4/4 time.

Double Tonguing

In double tonguing, it's important to keep the same embouchure and breath support as in legato playing. The tongue movement should be as small as possible. The fingerings must also be rhythmically synchronized with the tongue. The movement of the tongue should be thought of as a tapping movement from top down, instead of forward and back.

a)

b)

simile
c)
d - g - d - g - d   d - g - d - g - d   simile

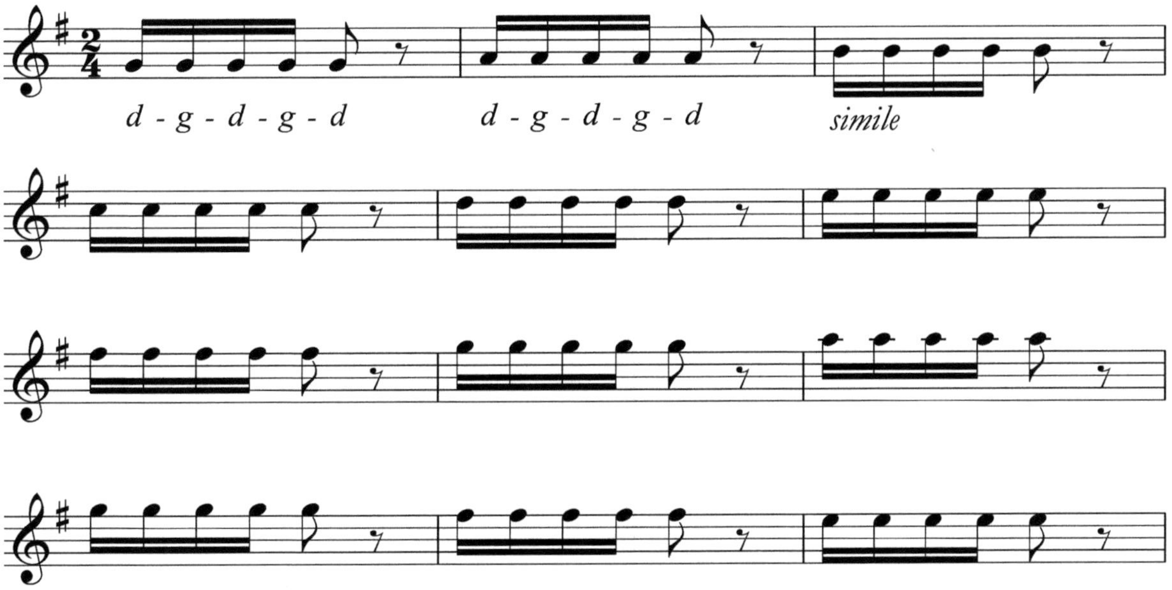

d)

Rhythmic Variations

- ◆ Play with a relaxed feeling and test both single and double tonguing.
- ◆ Experiment with the tongue staying more forward and touching the lips and tapping gently.
- ◆ Take small, quick breaths between eighth notes.
- ◆ Practice in different keys.

a)

b)

Rhythmic variations in 3/8 time.

a)

Rhythmic Variations with Triplet Tonguing

♦ Use fast airstream and small but active tongue movement.
♦ Keep neck, jaw and root of the tongue relaxed.

a)

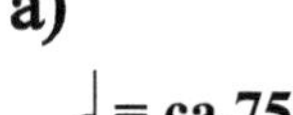

b)

c)

d)

e)

f)

♦ Rhythmic pattern from Maurice Ravel's *Bolero:*

 dvanced Tone Exercises

Pointers for Intonation and Dynamics

Basic Tuning:

Is the perfect fifth in tune? Check the following tones and intervals first for basic tuning:

(Herbert Lindholm: *Flautissimo, Pedagoginen Huilukansio* 1985.)

Crescendo

If you only blow stronger when you do a crescendo, your intonation will be sharp and you waste a lot of air. When you increase the volume, you lower your jaw slightly and relax the corners of your mouth, as if your lips were below your teeth. Thus, the airstream is directed more downwards and towards your toes.

a) Let it Grow

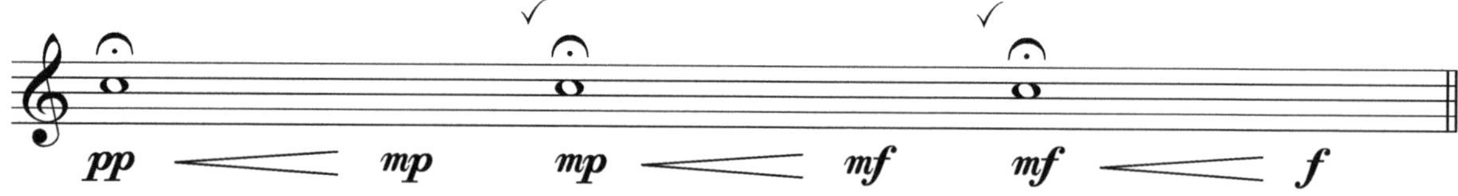

Diminuendo

If you only slow down the air flow when you play a diminuendo, your intonation
will drop. Higher tones might also drop into a lower octave. When you decrease
volume, you should raise the angle of the air flow and slide your lower lip (and
jaw) a bit forward.

b)   Diminuendo Lips

♦ Start by first blowing air towards the tip
  of your nose and then towards your lower jaw.
  Then try combining your blow into a glissando,
  sliding from the tip of your nose to your jaw
  and then back up. Keep your head still.

c)   Approaching Mosquitos

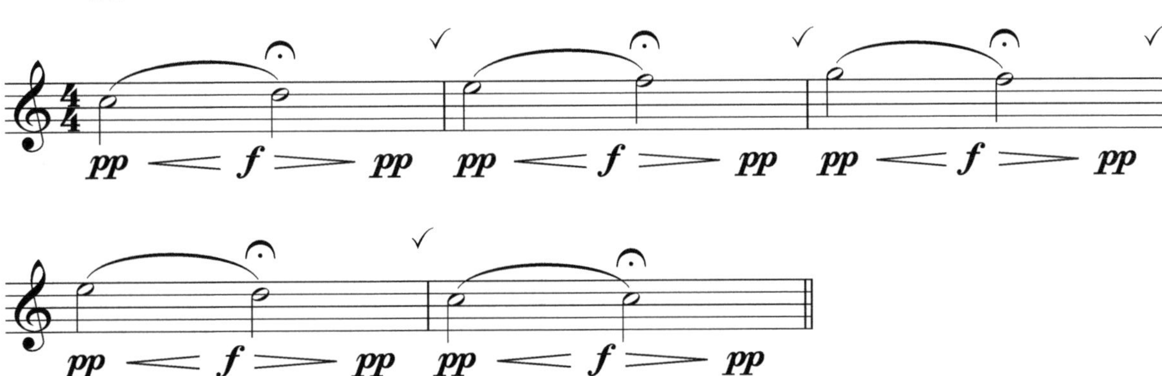

d) Mysterious Steps

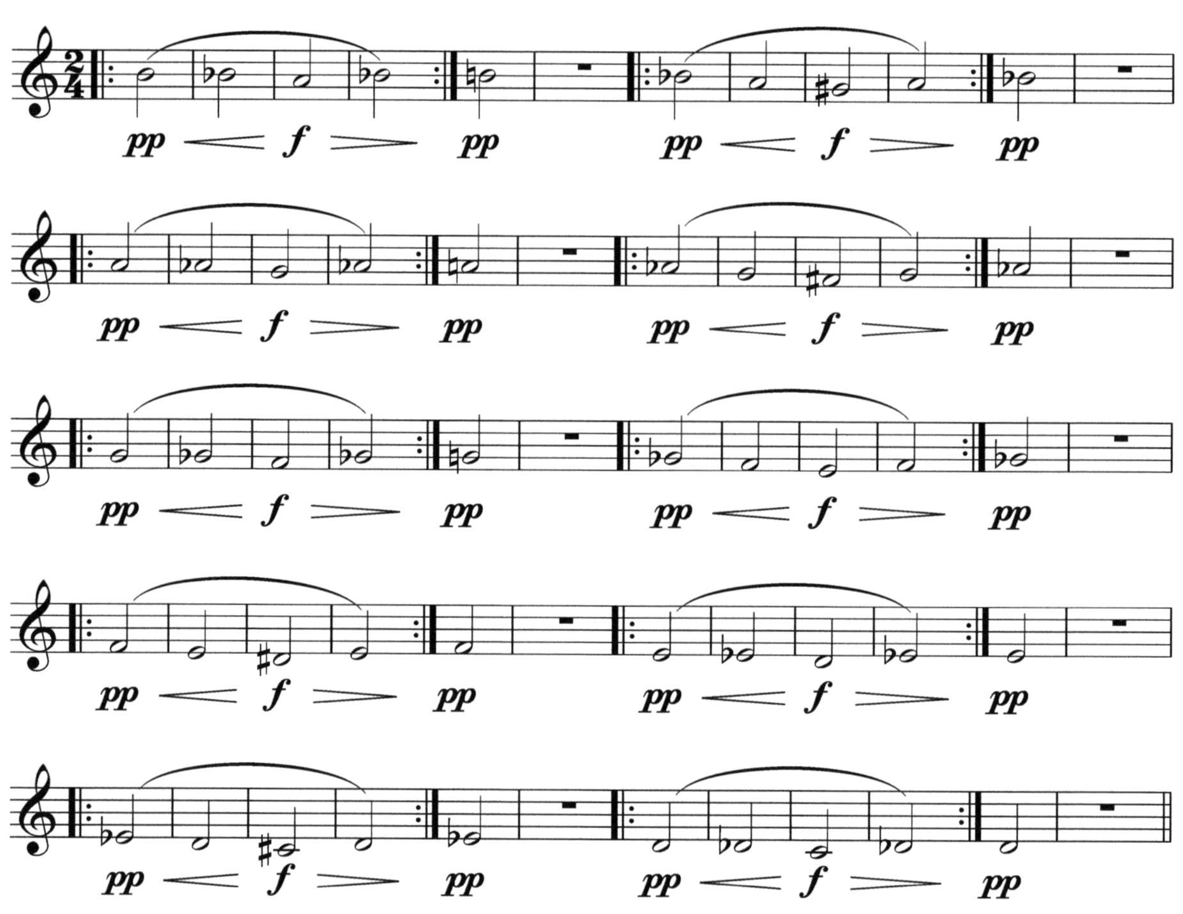

e) Secret Agent

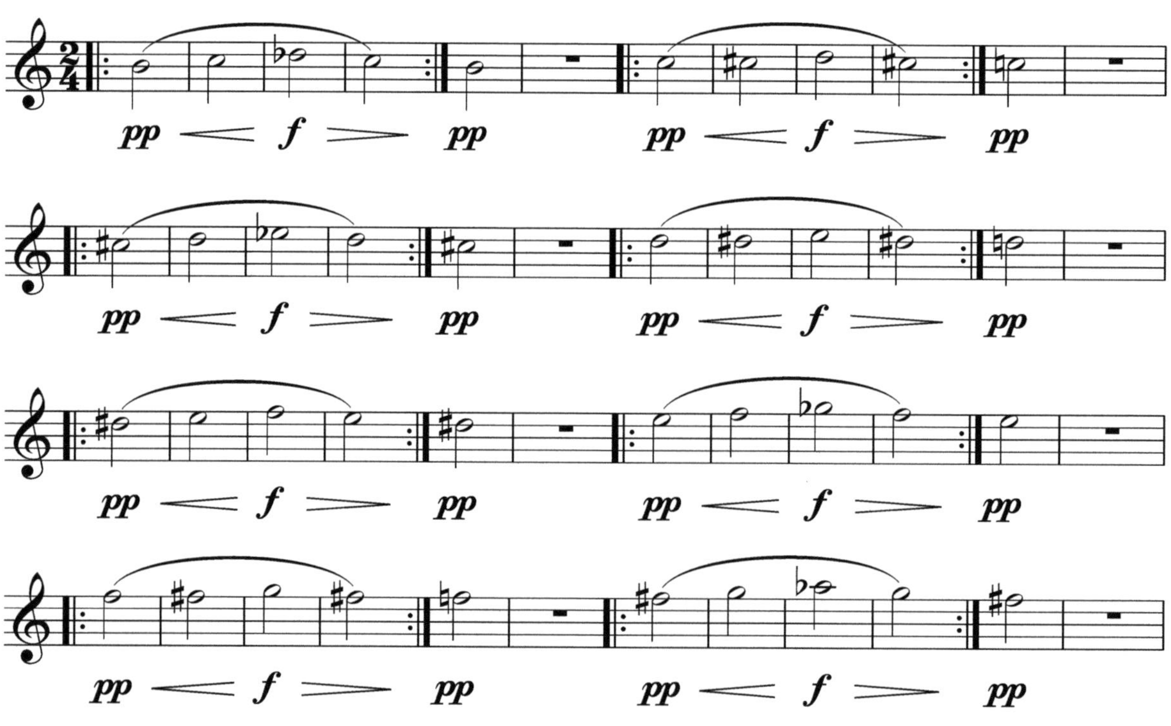

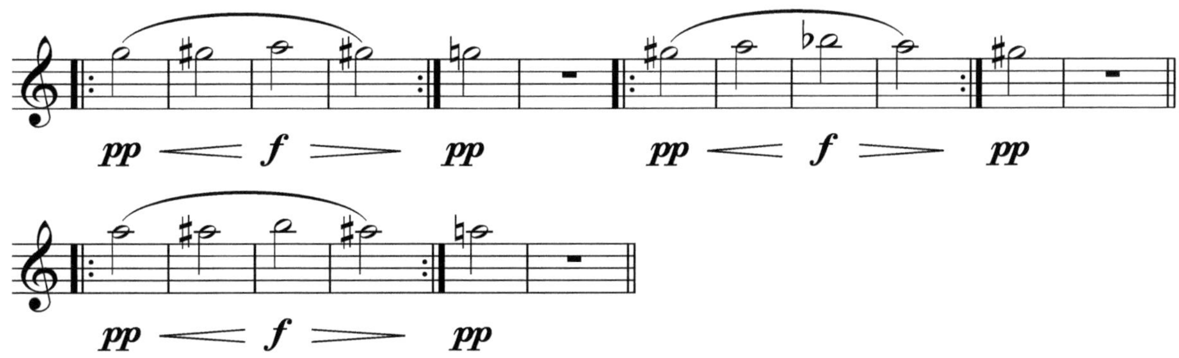

Adjust intonation by lowering the pitch

- ♦ Direct the air stream a bit more downwards.
- ♦ Imagine blowing air that's a few degrees warmer.
- ♦ Create more space into the mouth and between the teeth.

Adjust intonation by raising the pitch

- ♦ Direct the air stream slightly higher.
- ♦ Imagine blowing faster and cooler air.
- ♦ Bring your lower lip and jaw a bit forward.

A Few Words About Vibrato

Vibrato enlivens the sound and brings more glow and expression to your playing.
The main function of vibrato is to emphasize the musical climaxes of phrases.
Vibrato can appear naturally in the sound. When you play with great emotion,
often the vibrato appears naturally and as if straight from the heart. It can also
be practiced with different techniques and rhythmic variations. We can imagine
that vibrato is a wavelike fluctuation surrounding the center of the tone. It's
important that before you start practicing vibrato exercises, you can play long,
straight tones.

It's possible to produce vibrato in different ways. When the vibrato appears
naturally and without excessive effort and pressure, the movements visible on the
outside stay small and the sound is deep, beautiful and cantabile. You can learn
a lot about vibrato and how to use it musically by listening to string players and
singers.

Vibrato Waves

Relaxed and Flexible Bouncing
♦ Play without the flute.
♦ Pronounce the letter '*f*' and blow.
♦ Blow a "blast of winds" without your flute.

a)

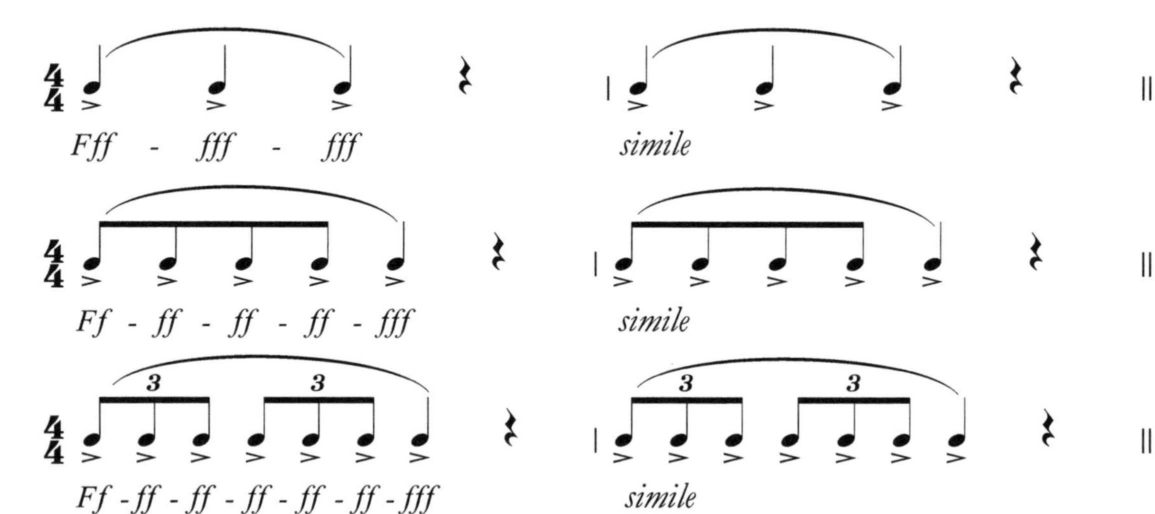

Triplets

b)

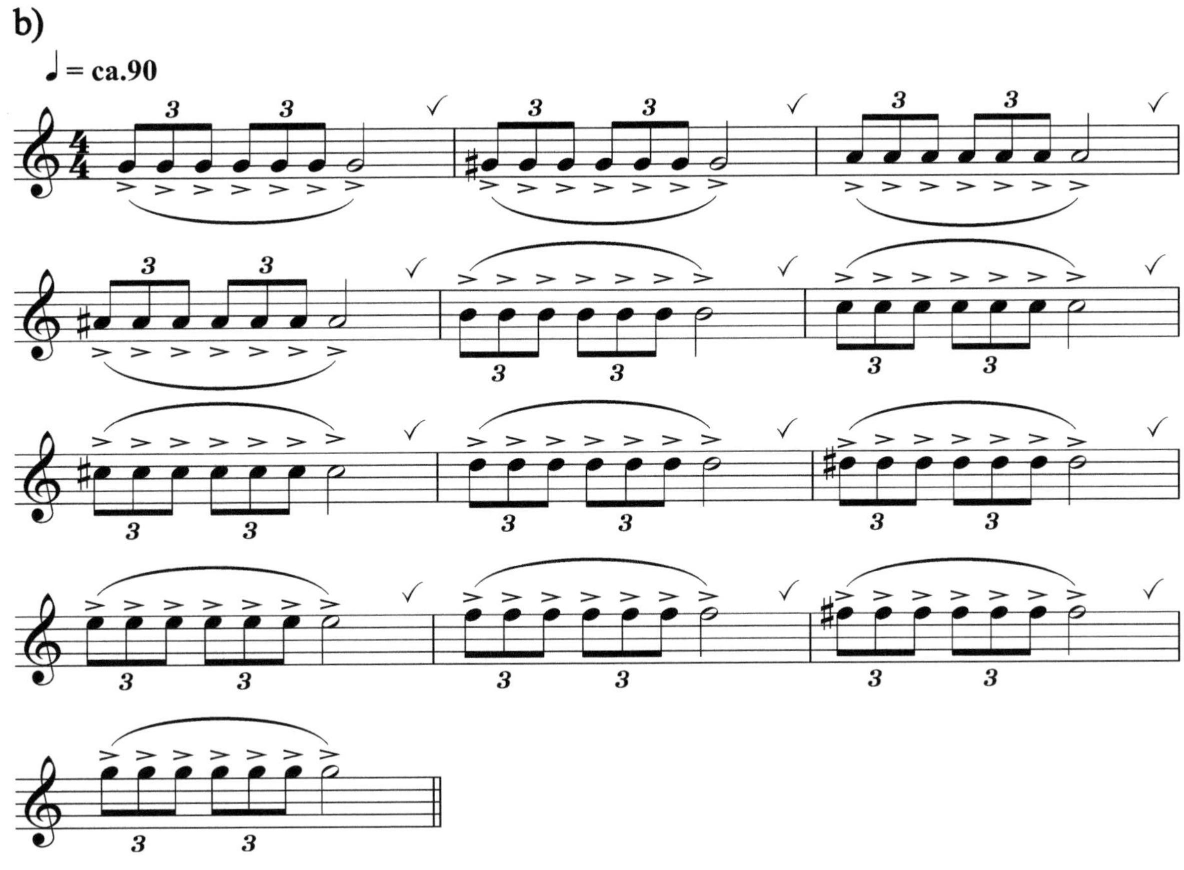

Combine:

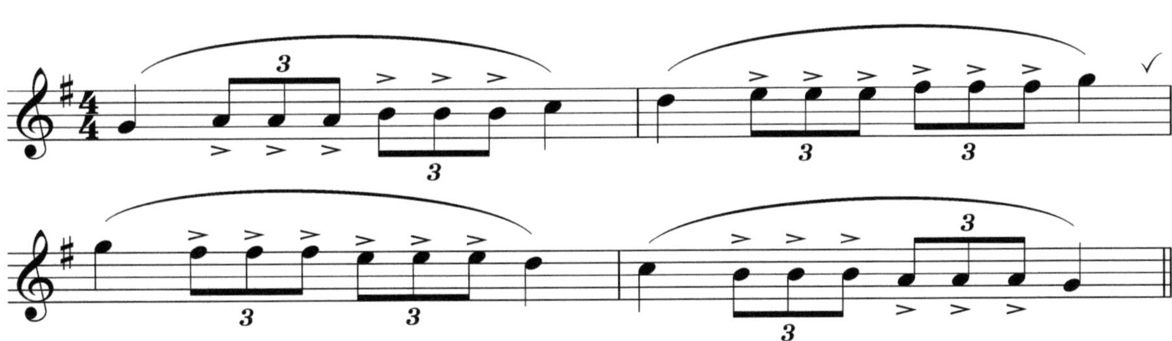

Triplets Down

- ♦ Freely flowing airstream
- ♦ Small, flexible bounce from a relaxed belly

c)

Triplets Up

d)

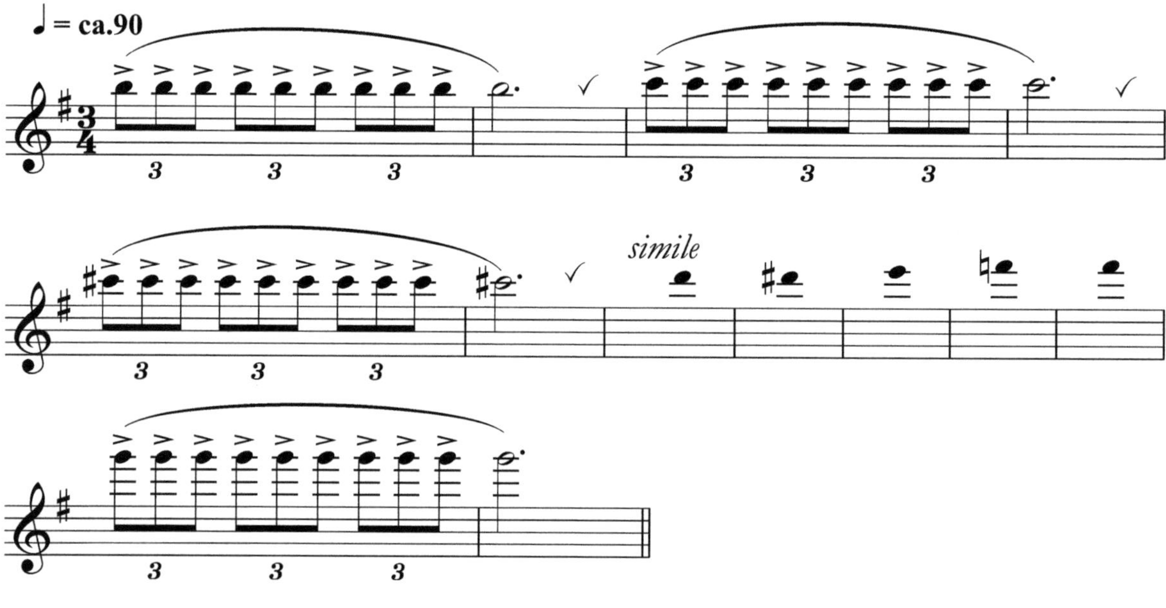

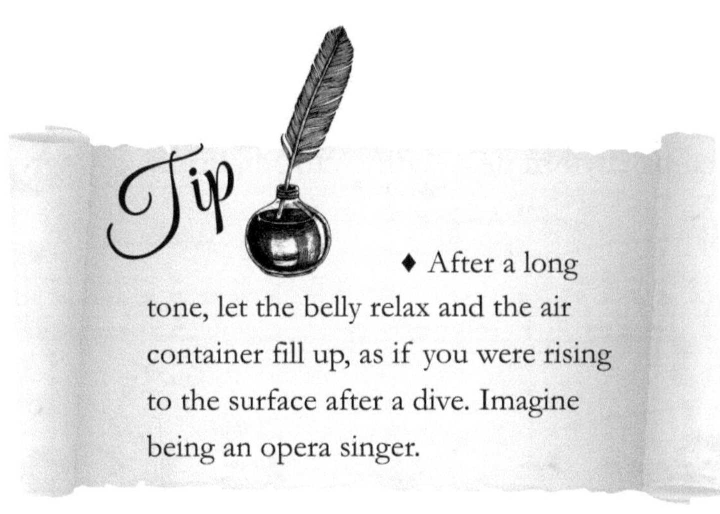

Sixteenth Notes and Quintuplets

e)   Combine sixteenth note pulses and a straight note.

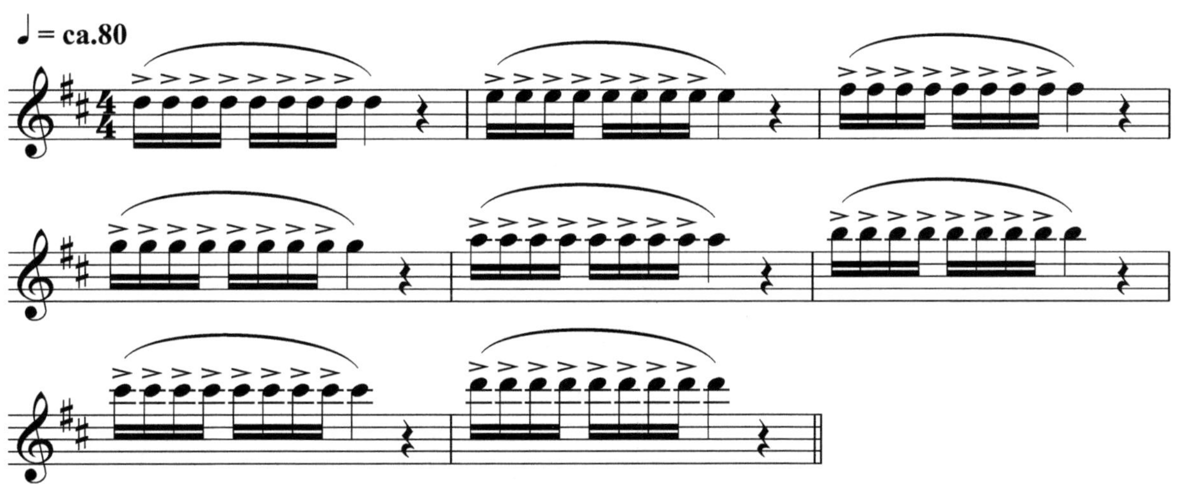

f)   Combine quintuplets with a long, straight note.

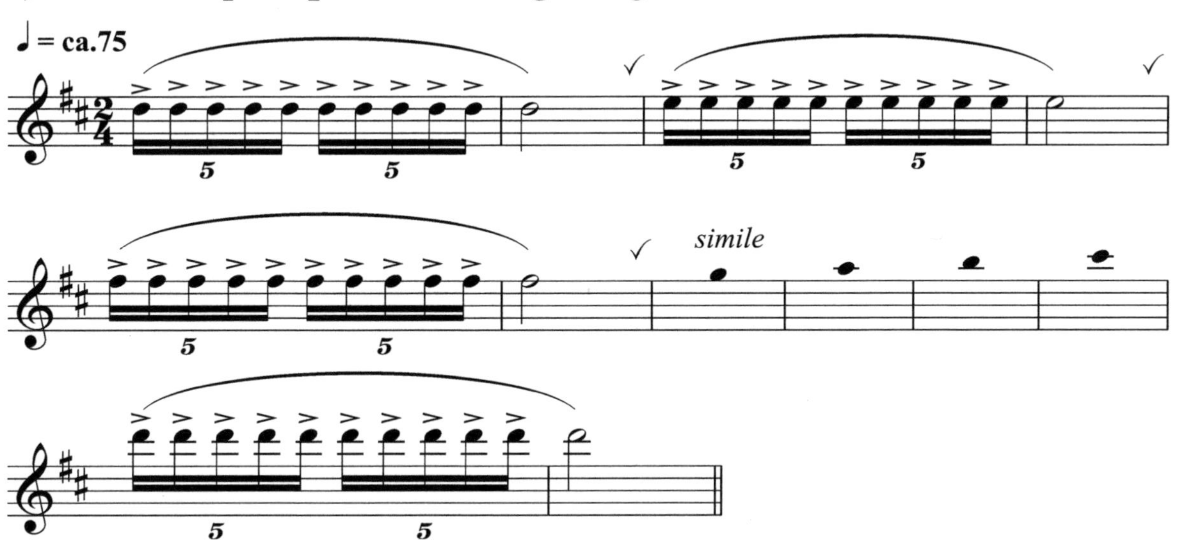

Rhythmic Chain

g) Gradually speeding rhythm descending chromatically

h) Gradually speeding rhythm ascending diatonically

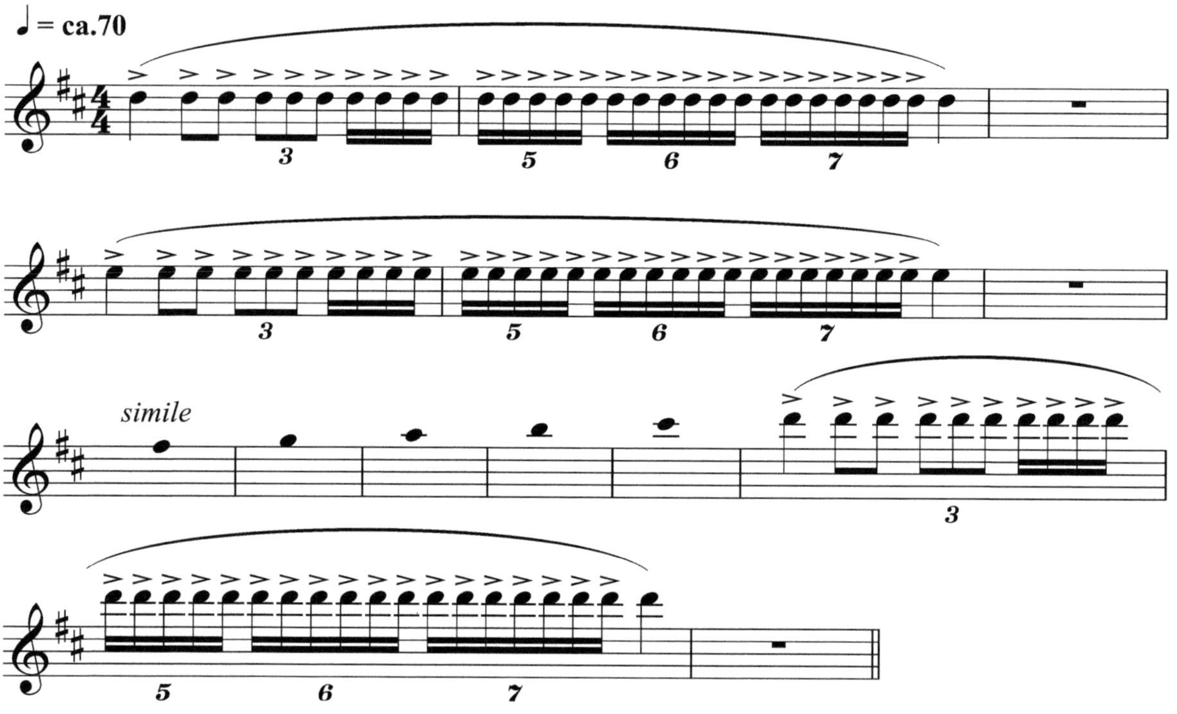

The Top Register Basics

The upper register requires a small lip aperture, fast airstream and good breath support. You reduce the size of the aperture by bringing the corners of your mouth a bit forward. The image of a vowel inside your mouth should be slid, for example, from "d**oo**r" towards "f**u**ll". This way you maintain the tiny air pocket between your lips and your teeth, and the "chute" created by your lips directs the air at an optimal angle, making it seem that the flute is playing itself.

Flageolet tones are useful for opening the top register sound. You can see how speeding up the air flow happens by increasing your support (instead of pinching or pushing). You can also use high G as a high register reference tone. Often when one discovers an easily ringing high G, for example, the rest of the upper register feels easier. The main thing to remember is that you don't need to form a new embouchure for every tone, but it can remain almost the same throughout the register.

- ♦ As a reference tone for the lower register, embouchure of low B.
- ♦ As a reference tone for the middle register, embouchure of middle G.
- ♦ As a reference tone for the top register, embouchure of high G.

Exercises for the Upper Register

Releasing the High Register

- ♦ Imagine an easy and floating tone in the upper register.
- ♦ Play with relaxed fingers.
- ♦ Play first in the middle register. Then repeat in the high register.

a)

- ♦ Up and down
- ♦ A mental image of the high notes on top of a large air cushion

b)

- ♦ Loosening your knee joints and squatting
- ♦ Leaning on a wall

c)

♦ Play like a tremolo. Keep yout neck totally loose.

d)

Copying the Sound

- ♦ Copy the sound of the previous tone.
- ♦ Play with different attacks, for example, *dew / hew / pew /* (leave out the /j/ sound after the /d/, /h/, /p/).

a)

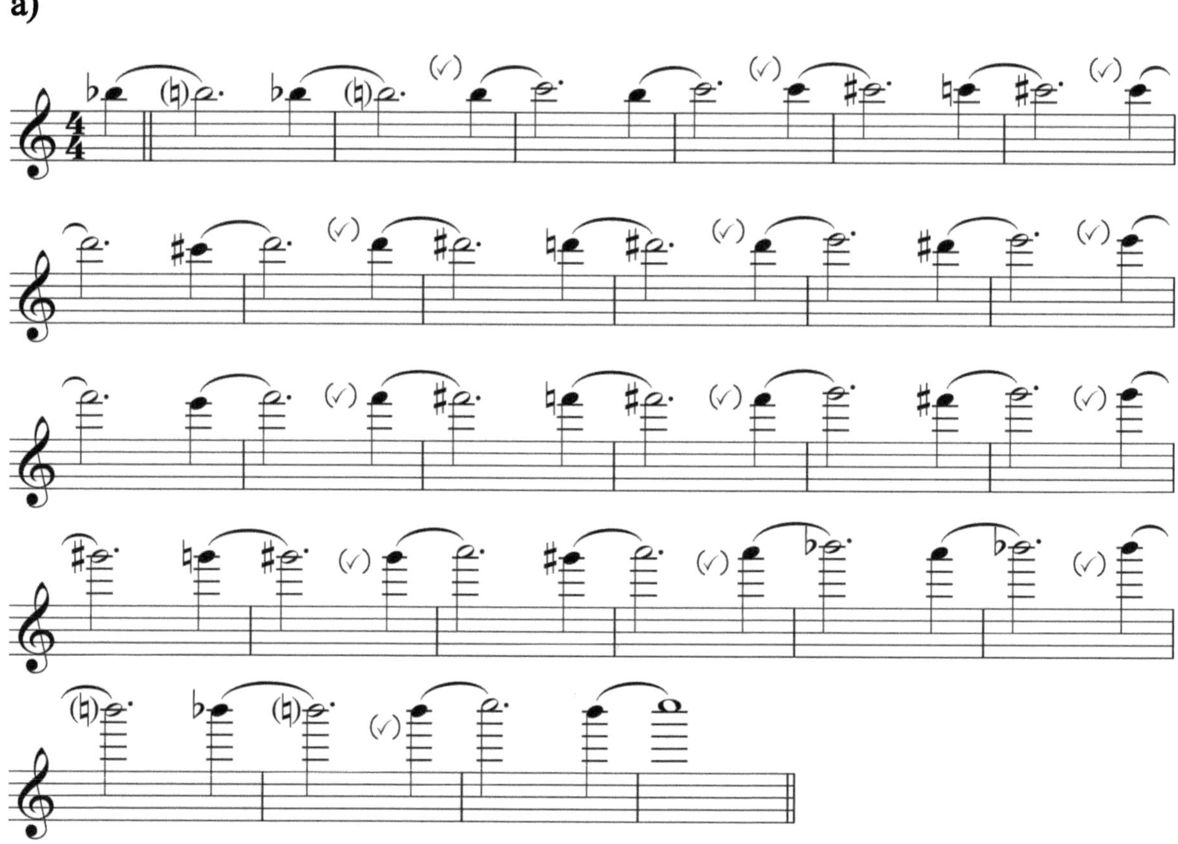

b) Chromatic scale with a three-note block

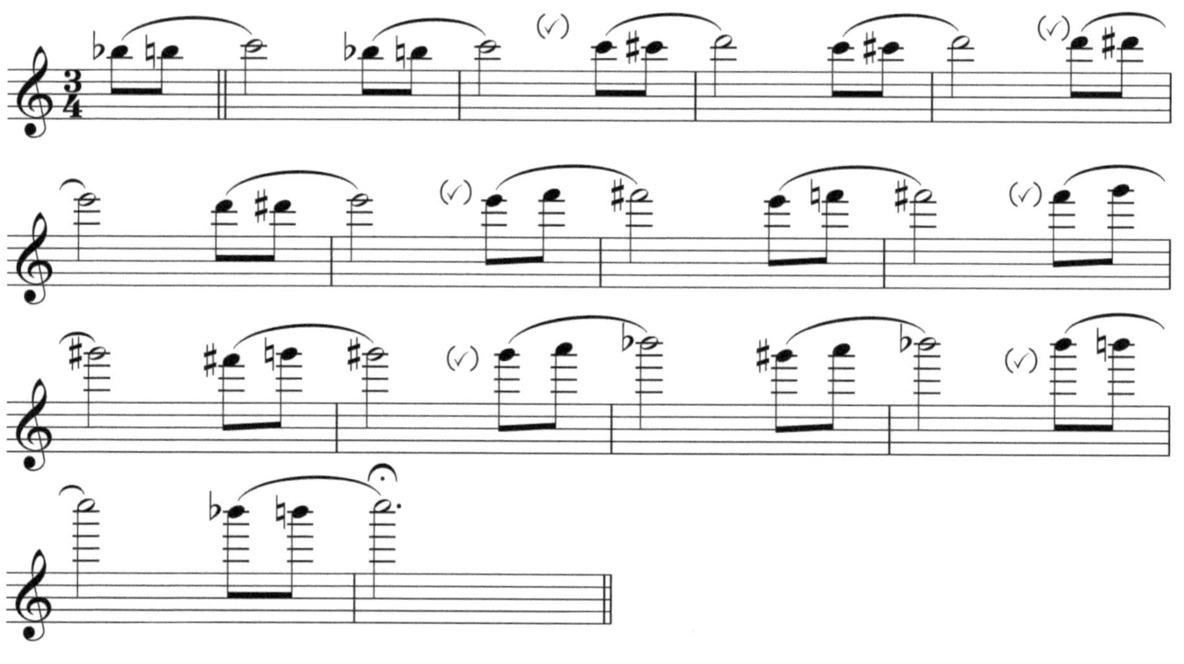

c)

Triplet exercise in the high register

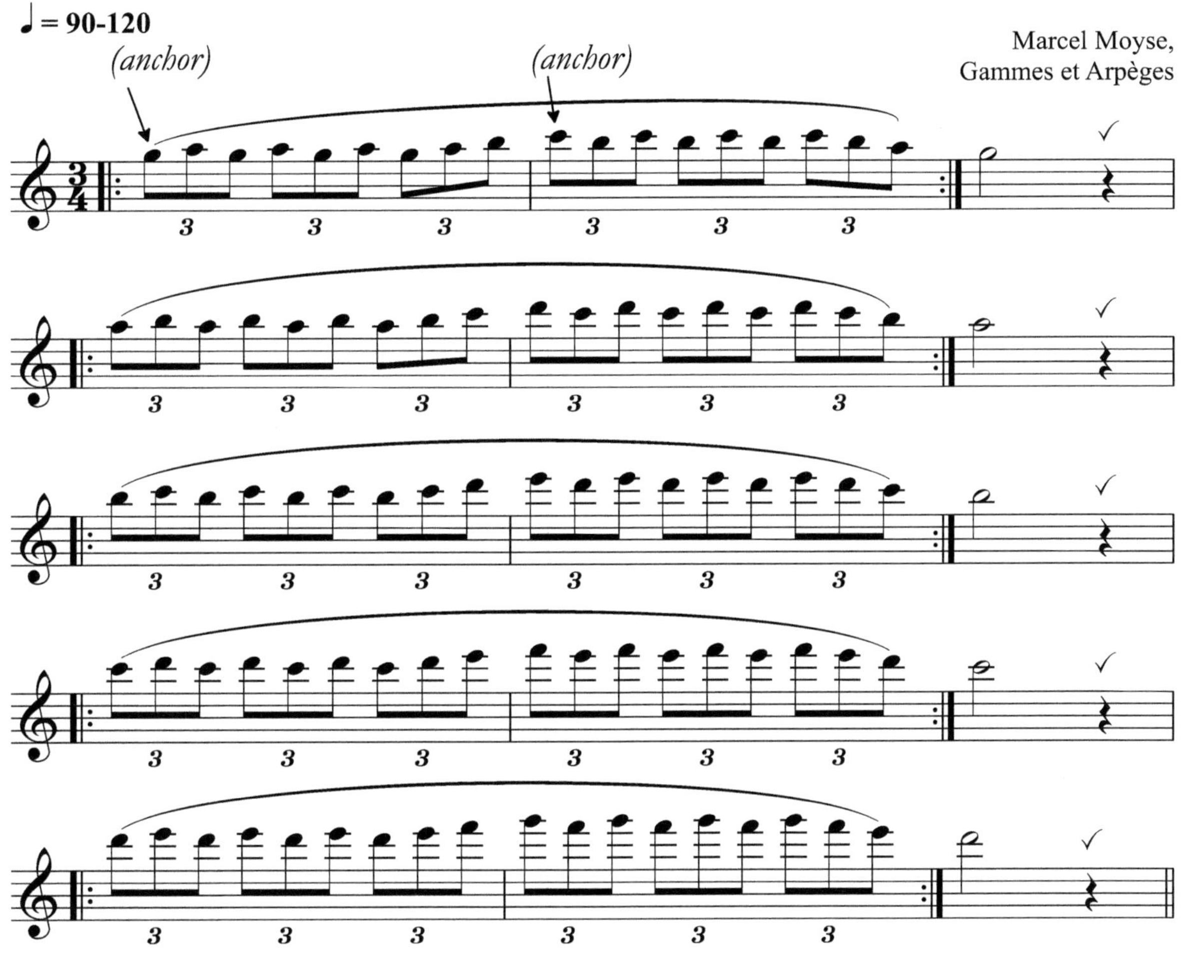

Chromatic Spurts

- ♦ Remember active and precise fingers.
- ♦ During the rest, get ready for the next pattern.
- ♦ Imagine the twittering of a tiny bird.
- ♦ Keep your flute steady!

a) Grace notes

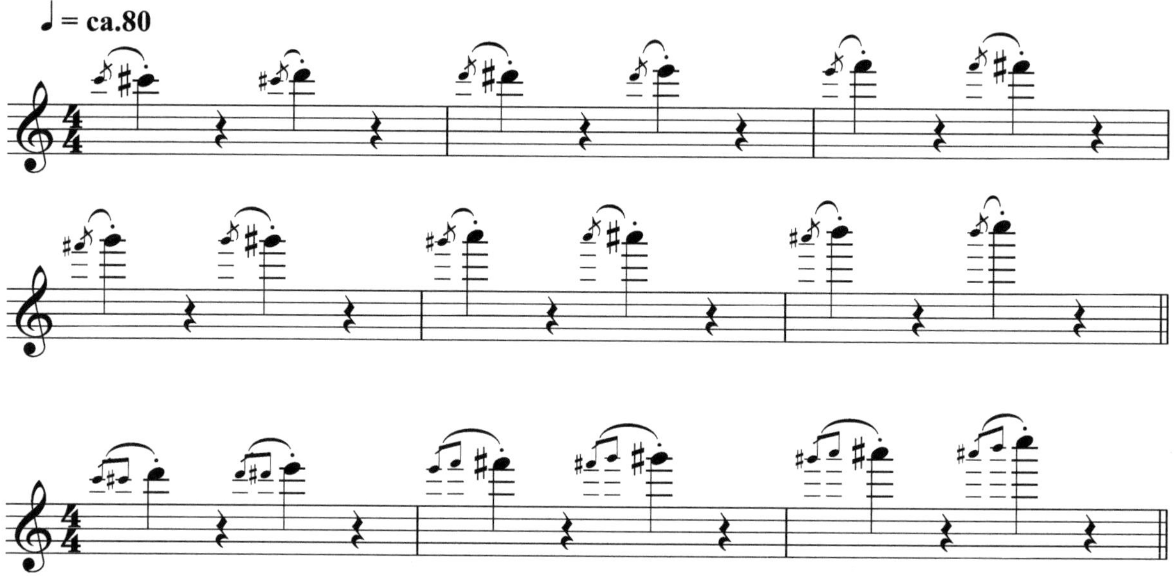

b) Quick chromatic triplets upwards

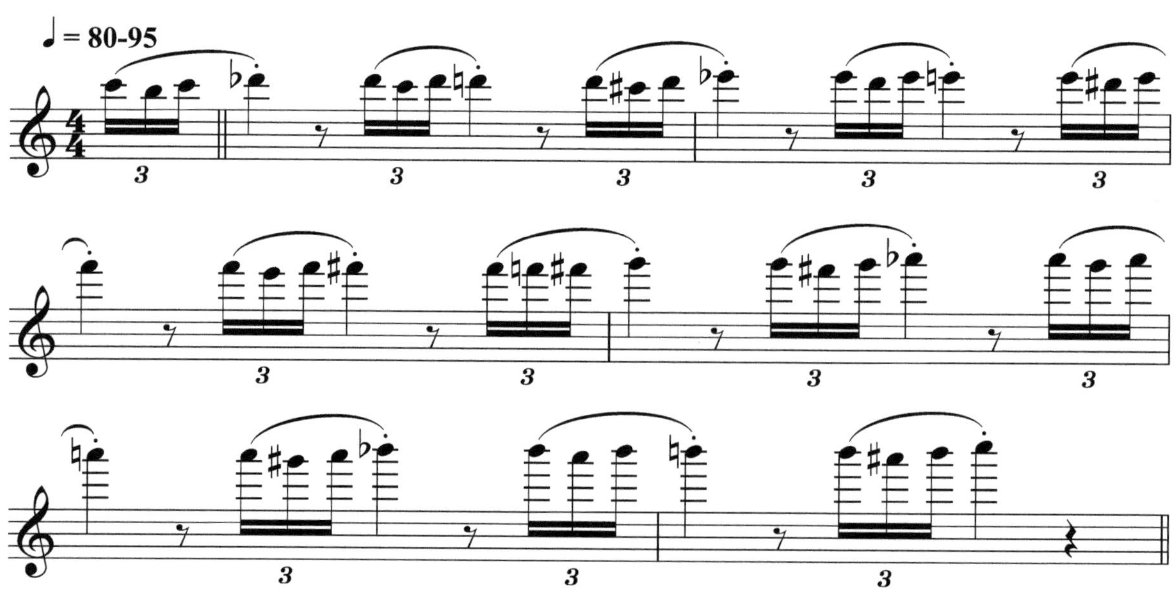

c) Two triplets upwards

♦ **During the rest, get ready for the next pattern.**

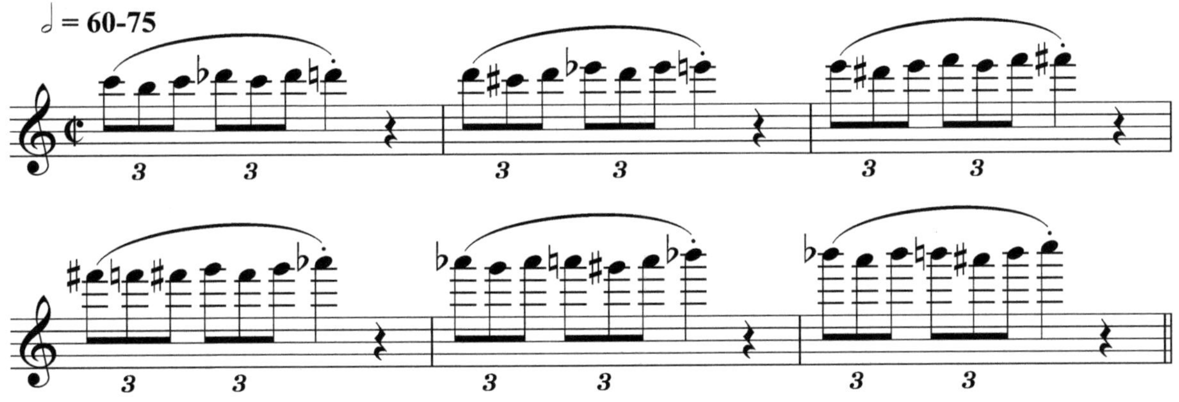

d) Triplets in chain

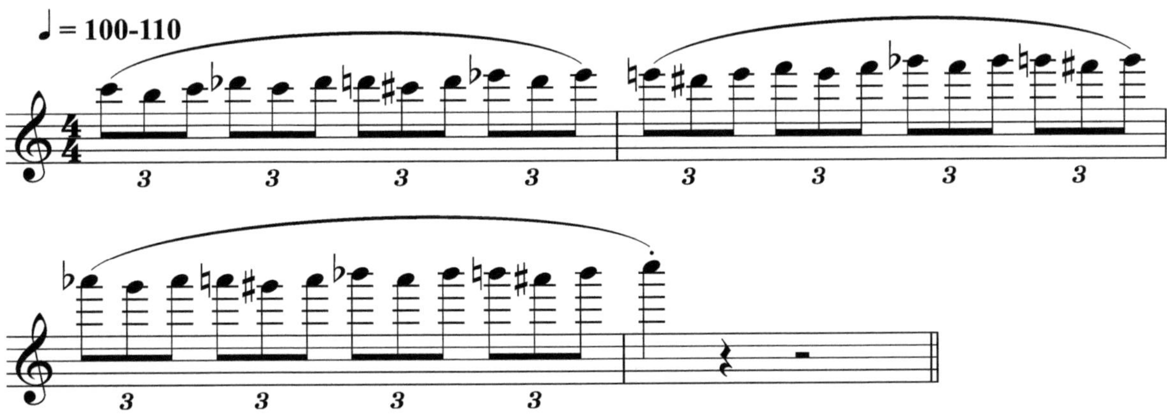

More Traction to the Middle Register

Cleaning the Middle Register

- ◆ Concentrate especially on the sound of middle E, E flat, D and C sharp. In this exercise they can sound metallic!

a)

Juicy Sound

- ◆ Imagine sanding down different surfaces with different sandpapers.
- ◆ Add a proper amount of traction to the sound while still being relaxed.
- ◆ Imagine that the phrase ends with a coarse and rough sandpaper to get resonant low tones.

a)

b) **Simile upwards and downwards**

c)

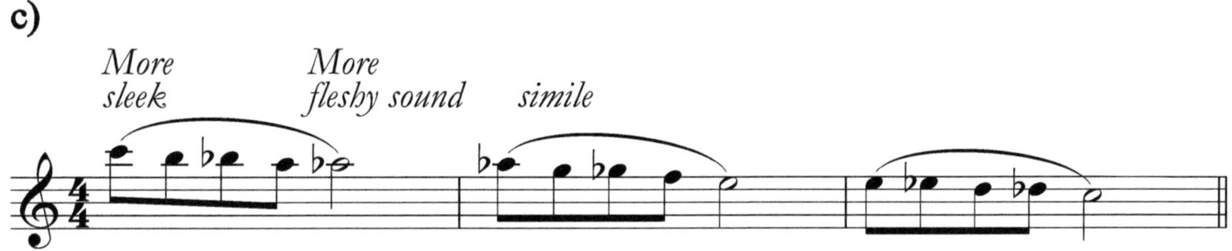

d) **Play a variation in 3/4 time. Maintain the tone quality when descending. Sound is relaxed but not too loose.**

Legato Octave Exercises

Tremolos

- ♦ Play elastically with slight accents.
- ♦ Play quickly and effortlessly.
- ♦ Imagine you are singing *Deh-ah, deh-ah, deh-ah, deh-ah, dah.*

a)

b) Tremolos in the low register

Investigate these leaps. Where and how do they sound the easiest?

Sliding Legato

- Use a mental image of a diamond drill buzzing.
- Slide in a glissando way.
- Look for a rich resonance to the sound.

a)

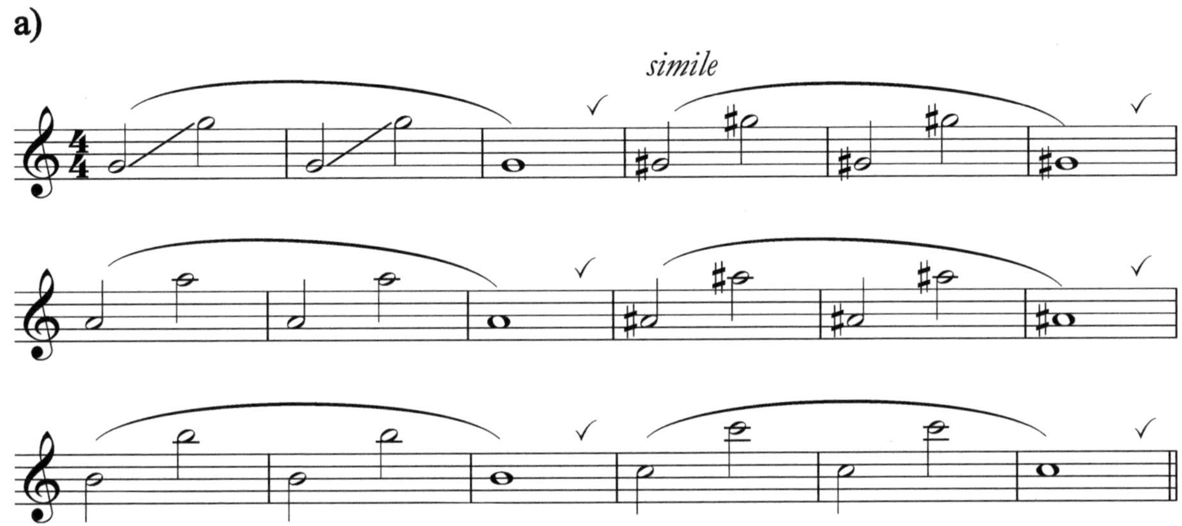

- Think of a beautiful swan landing.
- Employ the mental image of "super legato".

b)

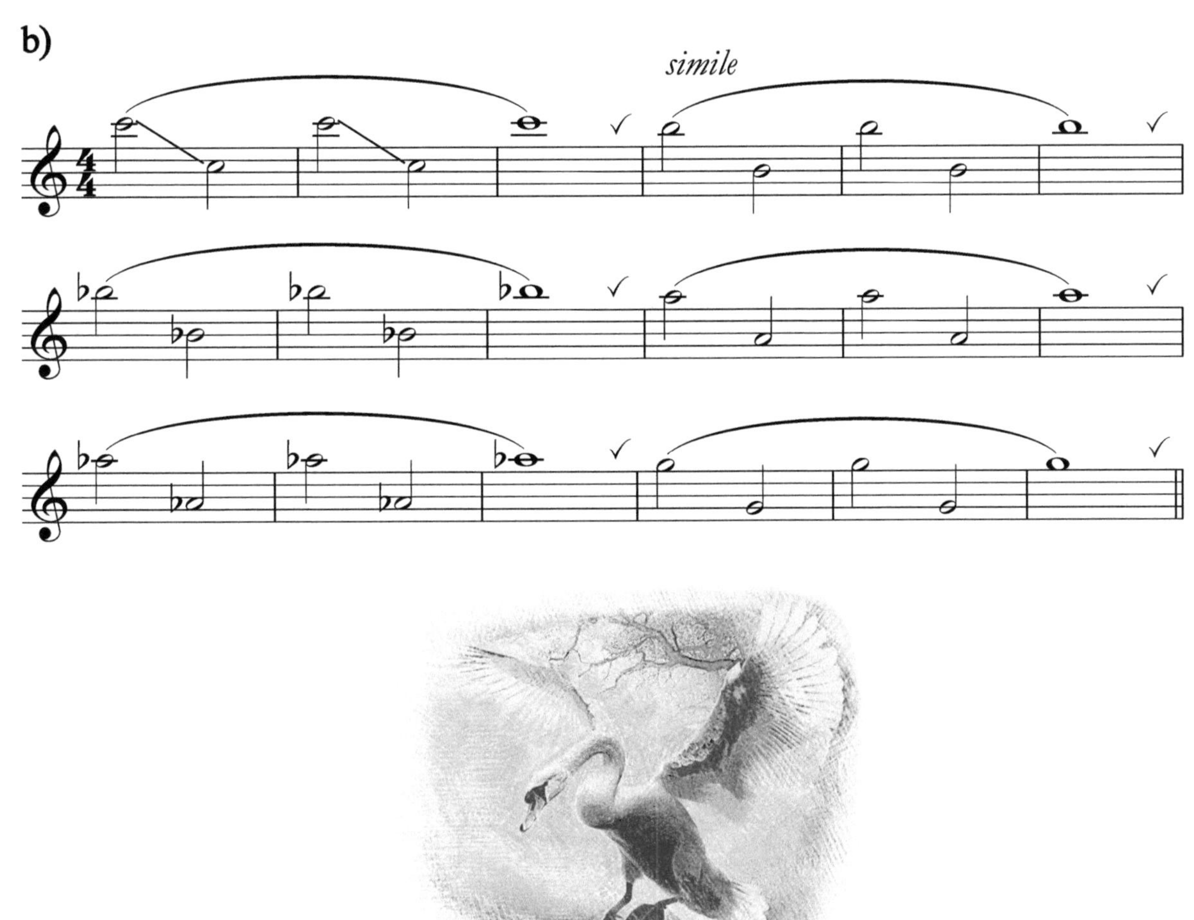

♦ Try playing middle C and high D
  simultaneously with high D fingering.
  Look for a spot where they sound together!

"Play with so much passion that the flute will melt."

- Rainer Risberg

Bibliography

Lindholm, Herbert. *Flautissimo: Pedagoginen Huilukansio.*
Kuopio: Suomen huiluseura, 1985.

Moyse, Marcel. *Gammes Et Arpeges: 480 Exercices Pour Flute.*
Paris: Alphonse Leduc, 1933.

Pearson, Lea. *Body Mapping for Flutists: What Every Flute Player Needs to Know About the Body.*
Chicago: Gia Publications, 2006.

Risberg, Rainer. Private Flute Lessons.
Lahti University of Applied Sciences, Finland. 2012-2016.

Taffanel, Paul, Gaubert, Philippe. *17 Grands Exercices Journaliers De Mécanisme Pour Flûte: 17 Big Daily Finger Exercises for the Flute = 17 Grosse Tägliche Mechanik-Uebungen Für Flöte.*
Paris: Alphonse Leduc, 1958.

Recommended Reading:

Cluff, Jennifer. "Free Articles on Flute Playing". *https://www.jennifercluff.com/articles.htm*

Graf, Peter-Lukas. *Check Up: 20 Basic Studies for Flutist = 20 Basis-Übungen Für Flötisten.*
Mainz: Schott, 1991.

Wilkinson, Fiona. *The Physical Flute.*
Waterloo, Ont: Waterloo Music, 1999.

~The Magical Flutist~